OUR AMERICA

AMS PRESS

NEW YORK

OUR AMERICA

BY
WALDO FRANK

BONI AND LIVERIGHT
Publishers   New York

Library of Congress Cataloging in Publication Data

Frank, Waldo David, 1889-1967.
    Our America.

    Reprint of the 1919 ed.
    1. United States--Civilization. 2. National
characteristics, American. I. Title.
E169.1.F82   1972   917.3'03'91   73-105512
ISBN 0-404-02547-1

129996

Reprinted by arrangement Jean K. Frank

Reprinted from the edition of 1919, New York
First AMS edition published in 1972
Manufactured in the United States of America

AMS PRESS INC.
NEW YORK, N. Y. 10003

I say no man has ever yet been half devout enough;
None has ever yet adored or worship'd half enough;
None has begun to think how divine he himself is, and how certain the
    future is.

I say that the real and permanent grandeur of These States must be
    their Religion;
Otherwise there is no real and permanent grandeur:
(Nor character nor life worthy the name, without Religion;
Nor land, nor man or woman, without Religion.)

What are you doing, young man?
Are you so earnest—so given up to literature, science, art, amours?
These ostensible realities, politics, points?
Your ambition or business, whatever it may be?

It is well—Against such I say not a word—I am their poet also:
But behold! such swiftly subside—burnt up for Religion's sake;
For not all matter is fuel to heat, impalpable flame, the essential life of
    the earth,
Any more than such are to Religion.

Walt Whitman. 1860.

TABLE OF CONTENTS

FOREWORD TO THE AMERICAN EDITION

During the War, France sent artists and men of letters to the United States to make France known to America. And when they had been here for a little time, it occurred to some of them that it might be well to make America known to France. These cultural envoys were of many kinds. Some came from the Academies and Schools: they stood for all that is traditional in Paris. Others were leaders of Oppositions, leaders of the artistic Left. France had the breadth to send this kind also. And now, quite naturally, there grew up among them a certain discontent with the official information that France was getting through the official channels about her Ally. These men discovered a whole world in America which, since it was barely articulate at home, was undreamed of in France. They thought it might be well to let Young America have voice in Paris.

In this way it came about that I was asked to write this book. Not because I was an authority: or that my message would be hailed by the Offices and Universities of the two nations. Merely, because it seemed reasonable to these cultural envoys to spice the mass of American conformist utterance abroad with a statement that could not even remotely be suspected of an official stamp. These envoys had come here, it is true, under the auspices of the *High French Commission*. But their purpose was to be as natural, as unofficial as they could. Part of their task was to discover Young America, to create channels between it and their own Young France. Wherefore, although this book is an indirect result of the activities of a Governmental Mission, the reader will find in it no trace of the "occasional" flavor.

The request for the book came to me directly from two of these visitors: Gaston Gallimard, Director of the Publishing House of the *Nouvelle Revue Française*, and Jacques Copeau, formerly Director of the magazine of the *Nouvelle Revue Française* and Head of its associated *Théâtre du Vieux Colombier*, which for the past two seasons has been playing in New York. *The Nouvelle Revue Française* is more than a Publishing House, a Theater and a Magazine. It is an organism. A flexible, rather sharply integrated organism since it includes creators so varied in mood and outlook as André Gide, Paul Claudel, Jacques Rivière, André Suarès, Jacques Copeau, Emile Verhaeren and Charles Péguy (these last two dead during the War). The *Nouvelle Revue Française* is an organism that justly stands for a great portion of Young France.

Now, I realized as I faced the task of talking to such masters, that the one thing to save me would be to forget them. If I looked up continuously from my page into the distant eye of André Gide, the chances were I should tear my page to bits. What France asked of me was nothing so definitive and vain as a lesson or a lecture. But France might be interested in hearing a young American talk—talk naturally—talk from his own viewpoint. And if this was my object, the best way was somehow not to talk to France—since it was not natural for me to do so: but rather to talk, as honestly as I could, to my own generation—which would be natural indeed.

Here was a dilemma. The comradeship, during two crucial years, of Gallimard and Copeau solved it. The initial move that released this book came from my talks with them. For if they were visitors from France, it was not long ere they were friends at home. Coming here from a foreign land, they inspired me to express feelings and thoughts about America—even to express a love—that otherwise might have been longer silent. Remaining as friends, they were capable of understanding. As Frenchmen, they helped me see America. As friends, they enhanced my knowledge of the single recreative Task which, in this *fin de monde*, makes of our generation in all lands a Brotherhood.

So they were a bridge between my needs. I could write a passable book for France about my country, only if I wrote it also *for* my country, only if I wrote it *to* my country. With them so near, France was not away; and yet my generation, my American generation could be forever present. Out of their request for a book to take back with them, I wrote words which I had long been brooding.

INTRODUCTORY

My dear Jacques Copeau and Gaston Gallimard:

In a real sense this is your book. I shall tell you why. You came to America and we were friends. You were full of the will to understand. You plied me with questions about my country. And I was full of the desire to share my country with you. In a strange way I was in love with it. I say that the way was strange, because the qualities in America I loved were secret. And all that she bawled forth with a strident voice were things that I detested. America was no sweet ripe fruit to be offered as it fell to my friends' palate. America was a hidden treasure. And to achieve it we had to blast through so many boasts, to drag through the morass of so many lies, so many myths, so many platitudes about America, that before long I found that you and I were adventurers together! Our talks broadened and deepened. Our words were by no means the reading aloud of already-written pages. They were a voyage of discovery. You from France, and I, were discovering America together.

I recall your first impressions, the early piercing of your consciousness by the steel towers and the shrill accents of New York. Seeing these impressions upon your mind, I had a view of the sheer surface of my country. I understood how false it was, its simplicity and arrogance, and how deliberate was this falseness, and how true a part of the American world it was, that falseness should cover it and hide it from itself. The whole vast problem of reaching down to the hidden vitals, and of bringing these up—their energy and truth—into the play of articulate life, came to me. And I saw that America was a conception to be created: in the painful labor of disclosing America to you by word and symbol, I understood how close this need lay to my heart, how I was in a casual way rehearsing in my talks with you the solemn rôle of all my generation.

America is a turmoiled giant who cannot speak. The giant's eyes wander about the clouds: his feet are sunk in the quicksands of racial and material passion. One hand grasps the mountains, and the other falls bruised and limp upon the lowlands of the world. His need is great, and what moves across his eyes is universal. But his tongue is tied.

We know the meaning of this. We know that utterance is a step in consciousness. We know that if America is dumb, the reason is that consciousness within America has not yet reached that pitch where the voice bursts forth and is clear and is understood. The problem is not to force America to speech. Such forced speech must be what most of ours has been: the parroting of foreign phrases, lip service to the maturity of England and of France—or worse, expression of the one formed and conscious entity in Ameri-

4

can life, the world of commerce. The problem is rather
to lift America into self-knowledge that shall be luminous so that she may shine, vibrant so that she may
be articulate.

So it is, my friends, that writing this book for
France, I write it for America—writing it for you, I
write it for myself. The effort of self-knowledge must
begin, to begin soundly, in the simplest terms. The
coal glows when every molecule is quick. My words
will have meaning only in so far as they express a multiplied experience: the gesture of self-knowledge in a
generation that shall, one day, become America.

Try, as you read these pages about the spirit of
our world, to bear in mind the body. Intense people
came to America as pioneers. The work that faced
them made them intenser. But America was intense
before the white man came. America is a land with a
shrieking rhythm. And whatever you would understand of our weakness and our strength you must interpret in this key. Centuries ago, a balance to this
autochthonous rapture was achieved in the Indian civilization. The Indian met the strain of his world with
a passionate restraint. Reserve became so deep a portion of his life that it can be no less than the need of
life which caused it. It was not ethical, not philosophical. It was an instinct for survival like that
which led him to hunt for food or to propagate his
kind. This instinct of reserve—a function of the
American world—the white man did not bring with him.
Much of the excess to which his ways were drawn in
the new life is due to an ethnic lack of preparation.

Even our climate is an excitant. Much of America is subject to great extremes of weather. Save in the low portions of the South and the South Pacific coast, bitter winters follow torrid summers. The range of temperature is enormous; and its rhythm is uncertain. The four seasons are scrambled. One may bake of a morning, shiver by noon, and swelter again by night. Yesterday I went up to the highlands east of the Hudson and lay in the warm grass and watched the grandiose river sparkle and slumber beneath his Palisades. To-day there is a driving snow-storm, and it is almost April. Such unceasing climax unsettles the human organism: keys it up: splinters the norm of nervous register into a flux. And the suspense of nerve reacts upon the temperament. The physiography of our world bears the stamp of titanic struggle. America is vivid and vibrant beyond the scales of temperate Europe. The Southwest throbs with shrill reds and golds of earth and blues of sky. Rocky New England swoons every summer in a purple verdure that cries against the browns and blacks of the soil. The entire backbone of the continent from the Canadian Rockies to the Sierra Madre is a chaos which turns the Alps almost to monotone. Rocks hurled like crumpled comets against the edge of a *mesa* they have swept smooth as a table. Canyons so deep that mountains are lost in them like stones. Jagged peaks flung through clouds. Rivers that plunge beneath the earth and reappear, walled-in by precipitous mile-high rock. Interminable wastes of thirsty soil, splintered with cactus, spread white with alkali or crystals of salt. Lakes that bubble hot in a bowl of brackish hills. Streams in whose bed gleam phosphorescent fires. Gashes like the Grand Canyon of the Colorado where earth lies disemboweled and men peer down into the stupendous womb of life. Such frenzy is the theater of the American drama. The behavior of our men and women inseparable from it.

It is this drama which I have endeavored to suggest. I write no history of manners, no history of letters. If I have dwelt long upon certain writers and artists, I have done so as the dramatist selects the most salient and most pregnant utterance of his characters to create his play. I have chosen and I have omitted in this selective impulse: to suggest a vast movement by scanty lines that shall somehow catch up the density of life between them.

It is a fact, however, that our writers provide the best expression of Our America. At the beginning, America stood forth most clearly in her statesmen. The United States, as we shall see, was a business venture: and politics is the utterance of economic life. The American genius spoke in men like Washington, Madison, Hamilton, Jefferson. The climax of this period came with the Civil War. Abraham Lincoln is the figure of transition: the last great statesman, one of the first of the prophets of a more vivid, religious American world.

Since his time, the energy of statecraft has been decadent. It was decadent in Theodore Roosevelt with his opportunist mind, his anæsthetic senses, his obtuse will. It is decadent to-day in Woodrow Wilson, who will perhaps be remembered as the Talleyrand of the twentieth century, the last brilliant brain of a dying order.

From the time of Lincoln, the drama of American life has shifted: has become the struggle for the assertion of life itself. And the utterance of life is art. Quite as naturally as the leaders of a yesterday given up to physical discovery and exploitation were politicians, the leaders of a to-morrow forced to spiritual discovery are men of letters. These men needed to break with the restricted reality of their fathers. They created a tentative reality of their own—the reality of spirit—and upon it our to-morrow must rest.

These pages, my friends, will in no way presume to a definitive judgment upon America. If you and your fellows in France desire authoritative words upon this country, you must turn to the academicians. For only in ignorance of a world so vast and so unformed can certainty survive. America is yet in the inchoate state where it has subjective meaning only. America is a complex of myriad lights playing upon myriad planes. As a Unit it exists only in the eyes of the beholder. Its reality is but a sprawling continent—mountains and gardenland and desert—swarmed by a sprawling congeries of people. To bound it is to stifle it, to give it a definite character is to emasculate it, to offer it a specific voice is to strike it dumb.

For us of the younger generation, America is a promise and a dream. Not a dream of infancy in which the real does not enter. The dream rather of young manhood to which the real *must* conform. We are in

8

revolt against the academies and institutions which would whittle America down to a few stale realities current fifty years ago when our land in all but the political surface of its life was yet a colony of Britain. But we are in revolt as well against that organized anarchy to-day expressed in Industrialism which would deny to America any life—hence any unity at all—beyond the ties of traffic and the arteries of trade. We believe we are the true realists; we who insist that in the essence of all reality lies the Ideal. America is for us indeed a promise and a dream. But only because we are sure that in discovering and controlling the complex conditions of our land, we shall find inviolate within them the promise and dream whereof I speak.

We who come to you through this book are beginners. Ours is the first generation of Americans consciously engaged in spiritual pioneering. This may perhaps be hard for France to understand. The homes of our childhood were still the homes of a people given up in thought and dream and action to the impulses of material discovery. Cultural America in 1900 was an untracked wilderness but dimly blazed by the heroic ax of Whitman. As the first pioneers who struck across the continent were men unorganized and isolate, so are we. You must therefore not expect that our America—the America we are discovering for ourselves —shall be a world entirely laid out, or acceptable to all.

I do not present it as such. But I do not deny, as I touch the vast areas of our land, that I find increasing numbers of men and women whose America seems

9

to be the same as mine. Our America is already the discovery of adumbrating groups. But it is true no less, that there are many Americas to-day. The concept to which adheres the greatest strength, the widest truth, must some day *be* America.

In this infancy of our adventure, America is a mystic Word. We go forth all to seek America. And in the seeking we create her. In the quality of our search shall be the nature of the America that we create.

WALDO FRANK.

September, 1919.

OUR AMERICA

OUR AMERICA

I. THE LAND OF THE PIONEER

No American can hope to run a journal, win public office, successfully advertise a soap or write a popular novel who does not insist upon the idealistic basis of his country. A peculiar sort of ethical rapture has earned the term American. Woodrow Wilson is only its latest adept: George Washington was by no means its first. And the reason is probably at least in part the fact that no land has ever sprung so nakedly as ours from a direct and conscious material impulse. The history of the colonization of America is the reflex result of economic movements in the Mother countries. Even that chaste gesture, Puritanism, sprang from the agrarian and industrial unrest of England. America was colonized because England and Spain were commercial rivals, because England and Holland were commercial rivals, because England and France were commercial rivals. Primarily, America was colonized because the spiritual energy of the Middle Ages had passed its bloom and was transmuting into the reactive channels of material growth. The dream of gold, the passion for silk, the urge of a short passage to the wealth of India—all the stirring envies of all the bursting European nations poured men and poured force upon American soil.

The first permanent colonies on the Eastern seaboard were grounded upon conscious purposes of wealth. Their revolution against England in 1775 was one of the first clear-cut struggles between bourgeois capitalism and the old feudality. The triumph of the colonies which gave birth to the United States marked the triumph of the capitalistic state. And from that day to this, America has had no tradition, no articulation outside of the industrial revolution which threw it into being. But because America was founded upon the rock of gold, she did not the less need her hope of heaven. The phraseologies of earlier European epochs—loyalties to Church and King and God—came with the colonists and served their purpose. Royalty was abolished as the rival of industrial exploitation, but the state that made Property sovereign commanded fealty instead. America could no longer brook theodicies. But God could become the protector of liberties in making money. The Revolutionary fathers first freed themselves from English creditors, and then bound down as their own debtors an increasing mass of the American population. The Constitution, which by brilliant means they thrust upon the people, secured the commercial oligarchy which persists to-day. But in the ugly crisis brought about in 1861 by the conflicting greeds of their materialistic

14

system, our fathers' sons did not hesitate to stamp
on their new-minted money: "In God we trust."
They were not hypocrites. Also they were not saints.
They were remarkably forceful men—the undoubted
leaders of their generation—who had no stomach for
kings and lords three thousand miles away. They
wanted to make money for themselves: that was what
they meant by Liberty. They were eager to rule
America in accord with their own lights: that was
what they meant by Freedom. Having found that a
loose Confederation meant loss to their investments,
and laxity to their control, they chose to band together in order to protect those interests and to ensure
their power: and this was what they meant by
Union.

The popular momentum, called forth by the Revolutionary War, threatened for the nine years ensuing
to upset the commercial aristocratic order which the
colonies had naturally assumed and which had inspired
the Revolutionary War. The Constitution of 1789
placed the moneyed Classes once more securely in the
saddle. A conscious minority of wealthy men and
lawyers, guided by the genius of Washington and
Franklin, Hamilton and Madison, formalized their will
over the small farmers and the nascent proletariat.
And from that time, America has thrived under the
control and cult of Wealth. As Professor Charles A.
Beard has succinctly put it: "The Constitution was
essentially an economic document based upon the concept that the fundamental private rights of property

are anterior to government and morally beyond the reach of popular majorities."*

Whence then, the moral tone that is never absent from American expression?

Men and women of high capacities came and were born to the vast lands. It is true that at the outset many colonies were stocked with criminals and indentured servants,—all the motley misfits of home.† The seeking of fortune in a distant and savage clime was bound to appeal to the uneasy elements of the gradually breaking social structures. But it is yet to be proven that criminals lack their share of idealistic and poetic power, or that the unstable and the poor are necessarily the weak. America, from the beginning, doubtless had her share of the salt of the earth. But what determines the evolution of character reaches beyond the mere intuitive possession of the individual. What dreamers and poets America in those early days possessed lived in an element whose stress was acquisition. The energy that parted the Atlantic and hewed the forests of a continent was wide enough and deep, to engulf much of the idealistic forces of the individual swept in by the pioneering Stream. It was but natural to find from the beginning a greater part of men's

---

* *An Economic Interpretation of the Constitution of the United States*, by Charles A. Beard, formerly Professor of Politics in Columbia University. Professor Beard is one of the many leading American scholars who have resigned, either volitionally or otherwise, from their Faculties for reasons which we shall later understand.

† John R. Commons in *Races and Immigrants in America* estimates that probably one half of all the immigrants of the Colonial period landed as indentured servants.

capacity for dream and for creation turned into materialistic channels—into genius for invention, for political manipulation, for accumulation. And it was natural as well that much of men's capacity for faith and piety should have become the slave of the dominant issue: should have evolved that moral tone at the service of wealth to which I have referred.

The stride of America was fatefully economic. Reformer, poet, priest had to keep step or be blotted out.

This uniformity of the American type is often overlooked by our own students. The mind reasons thus: Britain, France, Spain, Ireland, Germany rained their seed upon us. Therefore there could be no American type: but only Britons, Latins, Celts and Teutons. Nor can be, until the years have made the compound. But in truth, the Spaniard who came to America no longer was a Spaniard. It might be said that the inner character flinging him off from Spain already marked him there an alien. That leads us astray upon too intricate paths. It suffices to take the Spaniard, admittedly quite Spanish as he leaves Castile, and to understand how the great winds of egress that blew him across the Ocean, and the great blasts of adventure which blazed a trail with his body across mountain and prairie-land and desert, worked upon his nature: made him at length a Spaniard no longer, but something else, something American.

The American type at the close of the Eighteenth Century was as truly limned as it is now. For the unchastened continent worked primitively and brutally upon its suitors. The channels of outward-flowing energy down which the Pioneer was hurled were then more rigid and were steeper. Catholic from France and Spain, Puritan and cavalier and demi-slave from England, burgher from Holland, were moved by a common mastering impulse, were confronted by common, mastering conditions: and they answered in common specific ways. In manner and in psychology, the initial impulse and the experience that followed made these men brothers. They fought each other; they had no common speech; they made prayers and swore oaths each to private and distant Gods and Kings. But they were brothers nevertheless. They were that distinct and still unchartered creature: the American Pioneer.

Let us for a while observe how these primitive realities were bound to work upon the man who, for whatever conscious cause, had come across the seas.

He had, to begin with, to revert to a rough mode of life long since overlaid in Europe. He could not adapt the very real culture of the Indian. He could not continue in the cultural paths of his native land. He was compelled to call, by an unceasing effort of his will, upon every primitive resource. But he could not, because of these primitive conditions, become once more a primitive man. The primitive man is not the same as the man, fresh from the sophisticated world of Western Europe, who is wrenched back to the surroundings of a distant past. The primitive man moves with fluent comfort in the environment which has called him forth and sums his capacities of mind and manner. The pioneer must do violence upon himself. Whole departments of his psychic life must be repressed. Categories of desire must be inhibited. Reaches of consciousness must be lopped off. Old, half-forgotten intuitions must be called out from the buried depths of his mind, and made the governors of his life.

The early colonies lived in an unending beat of danger. A hostile people, a savage continent enclosed them. Their activities were narrowed in order to secure the intensity of resolution by means of which they could survive. Discipline among them was whetted by fear into ferocity. Pleasures became enemies and thieves. The early British colony of Jamestown, in the frenzy of its failure, fell into cannibalism. This was the sort of abyss against which the later colonies that survived were forever unconsciously on guard. The crude stockade that served to hold them against Indians and wolves became a symbol of their mental attitude, a token of their faith. Every narrowing instinct of self-preservation and acquisition tended to make them intolerant, materialistic, unæsthetic. Their own sufferings were the outcome of the vigilant control over surrounding life which alone could save them. Therefore, in their minds, their own sufferings were good. They demanded unity of life in order to face the unbroken foes that circled them. Therefore they were in no mood to brook religious or social dissension. Within the bounds of their domain, in their development, unity meant tyranny and absolute demands. Their sacrifice of leisure and of pleasure won its comfort in a rationale of strict asceticism. If they had no time for fun, fun must be vile and useless.

19

Finally, the measure of their world was one of watching: its sense was one of parabolic distances: actual motion was in the rhythm of their lives. The stern problems of self-preservation brought intensity to their inner inhibitions. And the inviting immensities of the American field suggested outward movement to their activities. The pioneer became a man, innerly locked up, outwardly released. He marched three thousand miles, but he kept so close the secrets of his breast that at the end he had forgotten them. His legs moved, but not his tongue. He was articulate in locomotion.

The spiritual power is man's capacity to feel life as a whole. It is that part of us which dwells within and yet may merge us with the world. The pioneer had brought such power with him: at least the need of it. It languished for lack of nurture.

Energy poured outward, poured unceasingly into material and practical exertion. Virtues which lent themselves to material conquest and to endurance were extolled: virtues which called for inner peace or levied energy without a manifest material return were vices. The pioneer had no time for vision, for that sensation of harmony which is the sense of beauty. He was too busy to perfect the relationships between himself, his fellows and the world. He had no immediate need to consult either his social or his spiritual senses. There was a specific acre to be cleared, a specific winter to be housed against. He had to abhor Wholes, in order to be equal to the infinite detail of his existence. He had to mistrust experience in order to issue continuously into action. Experience is a subjective matter. To experience takes time and meditation and an inner sense of values: demands the stoppage of headlong muscular activity. Experience was the foe of the pioneer. He had forever to be "up and doing." He had no leisure to digest what he had done. By the same token, he abhorred that vicarious experience which is art. To read of the voyage of Ulysses meant to stop voyaging himself. To dwell upon the terrible loveliness of life meant first to settle down. These occupations, therefore, became temptations of the Devil. The pioneer, in order to save himself from the sheer threat of being overwhelmed by his surrounding world, needed to combat it—its loveliness and passion.

But now this very fact of "settling down" confronted the nation. Beyond California lay an impenetrable world. The Caucasian, upon the shores of the Pacific, needed to turn his back upon the Orient: for the first time could not face Westward. The frontiers were clamped down. The pioneer's first Act was done.

But the rhythm of the pioneer ran on. His so deep and passionate extraversion* could not abruptly stop.

* Although the writer should be chary of the use of technical phrases, I believe the time has come when such words as extraversion and introversion may be admitted to the common language. The terms were, I think, first employed by the famous Swiss psychologist, C. G. Jung, in *A Contribution to the Study of Psychological Types* (Archives de Psychologie, Claparède—trans. from the French into English in *Analytical Psychology* by C. G. Jung). Dr. Jung elaborates on the "tender-minded" and "tough-minded" classification of William James. Roughly the *introverted* person is one in whom the predominance of psychic or emotional energy remains subjective, centripetal, so that the outer world must be directly translated into subjective terms to be apperceived: the *extraverted* person is one whose energy is centrifugal; whose psychic capacities and interests tend to rush out into the material and

Meantime, however, a new world burdened with its problems loomed upon the people. Old and suppressed desires of the soul were once more stirring. We neared the period of culture. The American body was well grown. All of its energies could no longer go to the adding of cubits to its stature. We were full-sized and we were huge. What we needed now was self-control of our vastness, self-consciousness, articulation. Lest we flounder in the world like a man with the mind and muscles of a child.

For long the overwhelming need had been the settling of land. Our measure for that work was good. The little energy that overflowed from the intense pioneer direction—into philosophy and art—was so minor that it required no measure, and it had none. But now the energy that overflowed was greater. Its tasks more urgent. By the old *rule-o'-thumb* of the frontiersman we had whipped the Indians and the British, flung roads across the Great Divide. By the old *rule-o'-thumb*, we now proceeded to direct education, evolve philosophies of life, write books, preach God, work out our cultural salvation.

The result was logical. The pioneer was master. The pioneer psychology had long since become the temper of the people. The immemorial loves of men and women—for beauty, experience, vision—spoke once

objective spheres, leaving the inner self depleted. These are of course mere defining abstractions. The complete extravert or introvert exists only in the realm of insanity. Most individuals have qualities of both too intricately merged to make the terms personally definitive. But as general terms of characteristic tendency, they are indispensible.

more. But they needed to be answered in ways that would not run counter to the rhythm of their world.

Here perhaps we come to the true meaning of the American moral tone. Immersed in a life of crass material endeavor, dedicated to a State in which the ancient services to God and King were lacking, the American in his protestation of exalted purpose was not so much hypocritical as *nostalgic*. The image that he conjured was of what he lacked. Deep in him lurked the sense of his material origin: a sense which his suppressed spiritual nature turned to guilt. He also wanted to serve. He could at least repeat to himself and to the world, in his every act and mood, that he *was* serving.

.   .   .   .

Edward Eggleston was a Methodist minister who, shortly after the Civil War, wrote novels. Later in life he came East and grew serious. In the American mind, this meant that he gave up writing novels and entered upon historical studies. But in 1874, he published a tale entitled *The Circuit Rider* based on his own experiences as a crusading preacher in pioneer Ohio. In this book an Irish schoolmaster is made to speak as follows:

" 'Now the Mithodists are a narry sort of people. But if ye want to make a strame strong, you have to make it narry. I've read a good dale of history and in me own estimation the ould English Puritans and the Mithodists are both torrents, because they're both shet up by narry banks. The Mithodists are farninst the wearin' of jewelry

23

and dancin' and singin' songs, which is all vairy foolish in me own estimation. But it's kind of nat'ral for the mill-race that runs the whale that fades the world, to git mad at the bablin' oidle brook that wastes its time among the mossy shtones and grinds nobody's grist. But the brook ain't so bad afther all. Hey, Mrs. Lumsden?'

"Mrs. Lumsden answered that she didn't think it was. It was very good for waterin' stock."

The words of Schoolmaster Brady express delightfully the subtle transvaluation of the spiritual energy of the pioneer into its nearest acceptable direction: that of utilitarian ethics. We are beginning to understand a bit about the ways of human energy. We do not know what it is. But we do know that it is like a river: that it flows endlessly and makes new channels for itself, and abandons old ones. And we know also that no fixed line divides the energy of man from the constant Sum which is the energy of all existence. We mark human energy only by the direction which it takes. We say of certain men who make great dreams like the ancient Hebrews, that their energy is spiritual. We say of others who build great empires like Rome, that their energy is political or material. Strictly, we have no right to make these distinctions. For energy is One: it is neither material nor spiritual. It is both—or neither. And religion and empires are merely channels.

Under the compulsion of the pioneer demands, in the complete absorption of the human energies in empirical affairs, religion became materialized. The mystical words remained. In fact, however, religion became an important aid to the business of life. We shall see in the next chapter how the discipline of the church became a means of marshaling men against the material difficulties of unsubdued America: how the denial of the senses released greater energy for the hunt of power and wealth: and how the senses, mortified by ascetic precepts—which so well fitted the crude conditions of the country—had their revenge in an unleashed search for riches.

The same utilitarian conviction fastened upon our universities. Most of the early institutions of higher learning in the United States had theological roots. And the close ties between church and commerce were annealed by education. At first, only a minority, the wealthy classes, went to college. Here the American youth was prepared either for those professions which sustained the exploiting social system or, more directly, he was schooled in a general academic culture all of whose meanings ran with the sense of the sanctity of property and the morale of "success."

Literature and the arts found their place in the universities. They found their place in the early urban life of the Eastern States. But there was an implicit understanding of what that place must be. "Culture," which the American had been forced to leave behind in Europe, became a commodity to be won back with wealth: a badge of place and prestige: finally a sort of bait for the catching of less wary fish. The bald truth of this attitude comes out in such institutions as the "Five Foot Book Shelf" first suggested, I believe, by President Emeritus Charles E. Eliot of Harvard, and later exploited by enterprising publishers.

Upon this little shelf, in essential and abbreviated form, the busy American finds "culture." Theodore Roosevelt is the author of a similar thesaurus. And to-day, numerous societies make fortunes advertising in the daily prints how the individual may achieve "culture" at the cost of ten cents a week, by subscribing to a list of "the best of the world's knowledge." These announcements uniformly stress the value of culture as a business asset. The newly "cultured" young man generally dines—in the advertisement's rubric—with his employer, discourses wondrously upon the Renaissance, the guano of Peru, the mistresses of Napoleon, the Pyramids and Ibsen. The employer is impressed by his culture and takes him into partnership. These appeals are not caricatures: they are universal. The utilitarian conviction rules at Yale and Harvard universities no less than it does in the extension courses of the Western colleges and in the widespread schools for paper-hanging and short-story-writing.

So also the one Philosophy that America can justly claim to be her own. We were at the cultural level where we craved systematic thought. We evolved Pragmatism.

The Pragmatic measure of value is utility. In our old schools, the full attention of all good Americans upon other matters had let hang on by sheer inertia a set of standards older than America herself, older than pioneering. To offset these academic ghosts that had lingered in places where the frontiersman had no will to go, any measure of utility could not but be good.

Any life is better than the dead. So in the benign hands of William James, Pragmatism became a tool of liberation from the old stocks, choking our colleges, of theological and metaphysical doctrine. John Dewey turned it, by his genius, into a stupendous lever that pried open the stuffy arcana of Education, let in fresh air, let in the reality of an intense American world. So far, so good. Pragmatism released from an ancient bondage. It now proceeded to shackle with a new. It was designed to wither away false values. But when it came to the next task of creating values of our own it emerged from its panoply of liberal phrase as a mere extension of the old pioneering mood. The point is that even this mood was radical and fresh in scholastic and academic circles.

The pragmatic measure of value is utility. At once, by this premise, the pragmatist, in a pioneer world where the concept of utility has become limited and fixed by an obsessive fact, loses all leverage *outside* of the reality in which he lives. But what America cried for was precisely that this reality should go—the sucking, shrinking reality of the pioneer. In this service, the Pragmatist was beforehand doomed.

Thus there grew up the general doctrine and application of the American Pragmatic school. . . . The measure of utility is the manifest process of Society, together with such individual acts as have immediate social currency. According to its pattern, the world is the paradigm of "getting on," of success. The values of life lose their inherency, become subordinate to the abstract conception of Progress, in which the world is

really posited as a sort of locomotive. Value, therefore, does not implicitly inhere in being. Life is a
machine, and like a machine externally produces. In
consequence, individual desire is bad, save insofar as
it conforms with the Machine's abstract activity. And
of course Reason is the pattern of the Machine. Reason becomes the *Ding-an-sich*, the absolute that the
pragmatists pretend so piously to abhor. Desire—the
emotional and æsthetic and spiritual capacity of man
—is Reason's servant. Experience, which is the sole
true norm of culture, the sole measure of growth, disappears: and the vast affluence of human energy is
channeled down (in theory) to turn the wheel of whatever mundane program the philosopher deems progressive.

Examine this creed, and its pioneer derivation becomes plain. The backwoodsman needed a rationale
for pressing-on: he needed to make the bitter sacrifice
of self, the sacrifice of culture, in order to carry
through the job of his Age—the unfolding of the
American empire. *His* progress was best served by the
suppression of Desire. Cultural and spiritual progress is a different matter. But however plain this fact
appears to us, it has escaped the pragmatist. Psychologically, he is still *moving westward*. Ethically, he is
making a virtue and a philosophy of his inner sacrifice, quite as did the Puritan who first denied nine-
tenths of life and then went about the land preaching
the satisfaction of denial.

The reality bequeathed us by centuries of pioneering and its industrial sequel made our great need the

creation of a new reality. But only spiritual force can create. Reason directs and conserves. Reason, it follows, was an ideal guide for the progress westward: and remains an ideal preservative for the traditional moods. Pragmatism, in its servility to Reason, is supine before the pioneer reality whose decadent child it is. As a recreative agent of American life—which it claimed straightway to be—it was destined to be sterile: destined to rationalize and fix whatever world was already in existence. The legs of the pioneer had simply become the brains of the philosopher.

Meantime, the popular magazines and journals were upon us. In their general nature which we can alone consider in this place they have conformed consistently. Literature, to the pioneer conviction, must not enhance experience, but must counteract it. For experience is a deterrent. And life is hard enough without the added burden of dwelling on it, or essaying to understand it. Therefore, even interpretation should be banished from the printed page.

Wish-fulfillment is the normal impetus in art. It moves in the novels of Balzac quite as clearly as in the tale of Jack-the-Giant-Killer. In the *Comédie Humaine* a great soul fulfills its wish to create and dominate a world of its own that shall, despite its subjective origin, be as real as possible. In Jack-the-Giant-Killer a fresh young spirit dreams of impossible adventures. Both of these forms of literature are healthy and essential. Balzac appeals to the mature: the fairy-tale appeals to the childlike. In the American story, we have a form of wish-fulfillment which is neither the one thing nor the other. For, while the American was active in the external world—mature and conscious there—his starved inner life stunted his spiritual powers to infantile dimensions. He demanded a literature therefore which should ostensibly deal with the mature world—the world of passions and affairs—the world of the *Comédie Humaine*—while his childish emotional capacity called for the spirit of Jack-the-Giant-Killer. What would satisfy him, therefore, must be a picture of the contents of real life, simplified and stunted to the dream-dimensions of the infant. And with just this sort of thing, our army of commercialized writers and dramatists and editors has kept him constantly supplied.*

There is nothing more horrible than a physically mature body moved by a childish mind. And if the average American production repels the sensitive American reader the reason is that he is witnessing just this condition. I do not refer here to the cheap *feuilleton* or the more simple motion-picture play, such as the Western scenes of William Hart. In many of these, the childishness is uniform. A naïveté flushes both material and point of view, quite as in the expressions of normal infancy. I refer to the artistic pabulum which the publishers offer to "serious" men and women, to whose discussion the literary pages devote their columns. The American is aware of the individual and social problems which inspire the current lit-

---

*Equally, the *genteel* writers of whom America has had so many. Preëminent among them, William Dean Howells and Henry James. See Chapter II.

eratures of Europe. He is conscious of the conflicts of family and sex, of the contrasts of poverty and wealth. Of such stuff, also, are his books. Their *body* is mature: but their mental and spiritual *motivation* remains infantile. The material is the complex reality of the world. At once, it is reduced to an abortive simplification whereby the reality is maimed, the reader's wish fulfilled as it could only be in fairyland. But the fairyland is missing: the sweet moods of fairyland have withered in the arid sophistications of American life. A child's mind in a child's body is a flower. A child's mind in the body of a man or woman is a revolting spectacle. And yet the authors of this sort of book are hailed as realists, their work is acclaimed as social criticism and American interpretation. And when at times a solitary voice emerges with the truth, its message is attacked as morbid and a lie.

It is easy to understand how optimism should have become of the tissue of American life. The pioneer must hope. Else, how can he press on? The American editor or writer who fails to strike the optimistic note is set upon with a ferocity which becomes clear if we bear in mind that hope is the pioneer's preserving arm. I do not mean to discredit the validity of hope and optimism. I can honestly lay claim to both. America was builded on a dream of fair lands: a dream that has come true. In the infinitely harder problems of social and psychic health, the dream persists. We believe in our Star. And we do not believe in our experience. America is filled with poverty, with social disease, with oppression and with physical degeneration. But we do not wish to believe that this is so. We bask in the benign delusion of our perfect freedom. In the same way, the pioneer, massacred by Indians, blotted out by malarial fevers, halted by desert and topless mountain, did not desire to believe in them: believed only in pressing on. There is this great difference, however. Physical prowess throve best unconsciously and fostered by a dream. Spiritual growth without the facing of the world is an impossible conception.

There are however serious sides to writing which America admits. Articles, for instance, on social and political subjects. For these have their utilitarian purpose. Their information can be applied. Many of our most proper magazines print essays and treatises of a high practicable order. Their creative work you will find trivial and sterile. The average American intellectual turns from a *serious* discussion about the League of Nations to a bad short-story, in order to be amused. I once heard a University Professor speak of a library in which he had an interest. "We have only serious books." "And what do you mean, Professor, by serious books?" "Oh, well—no poetry or fiction."

A very determined culture has held forth in the American cities for near two hundred years. It may well be characterized by the words of the Professor. The "serious" has utilitarian application: orders, organizes, conserves. The "trivial" enhances experience, nourishes the sense of beauty, fosters the visioning of life in its harmonious and universal contours, makes for the search of life in its immediate spiritual wealth.

There is a magazine published each week in Philadelphia. Aptly enough, it was founded in 1738 by Benjamin Franklin. For Franklin was the great pragmatist, the first sublimated pioneer of our tradition. This magazine prints varied articles on salesmanship, production, business management and success. Also it prints stories in which salesmanship, production and success are the true heroic virtues—clever stories, glamored with details of American manners and American Wealth. Finally, it prints numberless pages of advertisements, in which American Wealth sets down its articles of faith in words that are remarkably simple and well-chosen. Every page of this magazine— article, advertisement, story, with insignificant exceptions—is dedicate to the cult of material acquisition and to the suppression of any truth or any emotion whatsoever—even of any fact—which might interfere with the march of American Wealth. This magazine has a circulation of two millions. Its readers are not confined to any class or group of classes. *The Saturday Evening Post* is read by every one. The traveling salesman and the university professor, the farmhand, the capitalist and the stenographer read the same story in *The Saturday Evening Post*. At bottom, they have the same cultural, or more properly the same *precultural* ideals.

．　　．　　．　　．　　．　　．　　．

These are the cultural activities which have been completely stultified and redirected into the pioneer or non-cultural direction. Religious energy became first ethical and then utilitarian. Universities were schools for "getting on." A brilliant philosophy turned the old *rule-o'-thumb* of the frontiersman into polysyllabic words. Literature and art and journalism became lackeys of a possessive world.

Meantime, men of creative power kept on being born: kept on measuring themselves against the obsessive flow of the world they were born in. There were sheltered pockets in America where the pioneering flow was less obsessive: where individual growths were more subtly overwhelmed. They do not concern us yet. Let us go out to the naked and unprotected Plains where the vast Stream of external energy poured unstinted. Let us observe what happened there to the lonely seed of human spirit, sprouting against a flood. Let us face the tragedy, knowing it true. And knowing that if in this full swing of the destructive current we can find the tragedy transfigured—become victory and hope—we shall have won a knowledge of Miracle that cannot fail us. . . .

Among the men who made the magazines and books which, as we have seen, conformed so abjectly to the American conviction, none was more typical or brilliant than Jack London.

London was born in San Francisco.* Before he was a man, he had been oyster-pirate, sailor, day-laborer and tramp. Also, he had learned to read. By sheer drive of will, he forced his way into a Western College, earning his keep by working in a laundry. In

* In 1876. He died in 1916 on the magnificent California ranch which he had bought and improved with his literary earnings.

less than a year, his keen mind had tested the aridity
of such "higher education." He applied for a place as
postman. And while he waited for his appointment, he
wrote some stories which he managed to sell. From
that time on, he decided—to paraphrase his words—
no longer to earn his bread by brawn when brains
seemed to serve him so much better.

Now, the background of this gifted man was the
background of America. He had gone back to primal
stratum: stolen and labored and adventured. Finally,
he had learned to write. Criticism grew in him. He
pierced the American myths. He no longer believed in
the Puritan God. He no longer believed in the Constitution. He signed his personal letters "yours for
the Revolution." But what of this experience and passion and exploration lives in his books? Precisely,
nothing. London became a "best-seller." He sold himself to a Syndicate which paid him a fabulous price for
every word he wrote. He visited half the world, and
produced a thousand words a day. And the burden
of his literary output was an infantile romanticism under which he deliberately hid his own despair. Since
the reality of the world he had come up through was
barred to his pen, he wrote stories about sea-wolves and
star-gazers: he wallowed in the details of bloody combat. If he was aware of the density of American life,
of the drama of the conflict of its planes, he used his
knowledge only as a measure of avoidance. He claimed
to have found truth in a complete cynical disillusion.
"But I know better," he says, "than to give this truth

as I have seen it, in my books. The bubbles of illusion, the pap of pretty lies are the true stuff of stories."

Of course, a man so at odds with his experience could not compose a true autobiography. But in one of London's later volumes, *John Barleycorn*, there is the essence of confession. To the psychologist, a lie is as true a testimony as a consciously stated fact: for it is the word of the unconscious wish. So in this book, London professes to trace the growth of his love for drink under the guise of setting himself forth as an object lesson to the world, and merely portrays the bully and the playboy. Page after page we follow London through the pathos and splendor of his days: and learn that he learned nothing by them. His book reveals no trace of self-consciousness, no suggestion of the sanctity of art, no hint of the values of life. Almost it seems that the violent activities of London's youth had sapped that reservoir of inner force by which consciousness, the impulse toward truth, are nurtured.

In this, the analogy between the author and America is clear. London was an over-extraverted man. Propelled through the external world, he drew upon the energies that normally remain within to effect his progress. He was conscious of the external world merely as a fact to be traversed, as material to be exploited. There remained no base of inner energy to make him conscious of self. He had in consequence no source of knowledge to which to bring his experience of life, and make life conscious also. He lacked the inner fire to light up a single phase of the American scene. The American scene remained a sodden, ugly substance.

London by nature was a self-conscious, socially conscious man. He could have found himself only in a sort of immediate expression that clinched the problems of his day. But the *taboo* of an extraverted world against mature experience barred him. He dared not live in the reality of the present: he fell back on the reality of childhood. The best of London went into tales of the past frontier—the national childhood: into tales of wolves and dogs—the infancy of sense.

The extraverted man relies on outer props, since he himself is depleted. He finds the reason for his ills in the external world: seeks their cure in outward means. Thus, the American State passes laws, where the Oriental exhorts the soul. Legislation becomes a substitute for grace. Similarly, Jack London unconsciously unfolds the tale of his starved soul among these mazes of adventure, and describes how at last drink took the place of the inner stimulus which he had somehow lost. He is keen enough to feel the normality of his despair. But his cure for it is Prohibition! London drank. America passes the Constitutional Amendment.

Like his country, Jack London was corporeally mature, innerly a child. He mastered the outward circumstance of life—and then played with toys. The world was his, by physical and intellectual possession: but he preferred to live in a nursery, and blamed his excess drinking on the fact that no Nurse was there to keep the liquor from his lips. A dangerous analogue, his life, to the career of a nation that pursues the same dual course of material aggrandizement and spiritual abolition.*

But the land of the pioneer has had a more heroic victim. Jack London was a man of talent: Mark Twain was a man of genius. The mind of Jack London was brilliant: the soul of Mark Twain was great. . . .

Out of the bitter wreckage of his long life, one great work emerges by whose contrasting fire we can observe the darkness. This work is *Huckleberry Finn*. It must go down in history, not as the expression of a rich national culture like the books of Chaucer, Rabelais, Cervantes, but as the voice of American chaos, the voice of a precultural epoch. Mark Twain kept this book long at his side. Ostensibly, it was the sequel to *The Adventures of Tom Sawyer* which appeared in 1875. "Huck" came nine years later. In it for once, the soul of Mark Twain burst its bonds of false instruction and false ideal, and found voice. Mark Twain lived twenty-six years longer. That voice never spoke again.

Huckleberry Finn is the simple story of a young white lad, born on the banks of the Mississippi who, with an escaped slave named Jim, builds a raft and

* Very shortly before his death, I received a letter from Jack London, part of which I think I may quote here without indiscretion, as indicative of the inner helplessness of the man and of his too late realization. I had been informed by friends that London had written some really good stories which, because of their value, were valueless to the wealthy magazines for which he regularly wrote. If such stories existed, I wanted them for the magazine of which I was then an editor. Mr. London wrote me that such stories did not exist. "I do not mind telling you," he concluded, "that had the United States been as kindly toward the short story writer as France has always been kindly, from the beginning of my writing career I would have written many a score of short stories quite different from the ones I have written."

floats down the mighty current. Mark Twain originally had meant it to be nothing else: had meant it for the mere sequel of another tale. But his theme was too apt a symbol. Into it he poured his soul.

Huck is a candid ignorant courageous child. He is full of the cunning and virtue of the resilient savage. He wears the habiliments of the civilization from which he comes, loosely, like trinkets about his neck. He and his companion build a raft and float. At night they veer their craft into the shallows or sleep on land. They have many adventures. The adventures that Huck has are the material of pioneering life. He always *happens* upon them. At times, he is a mere spectator: at time enforced accessory. Always, he is passive before a vaster fact. Huck is America. And Huck *floats* down the current of a mighty Stream.

Huckleberry Finn is the American epic hero. Greece had Ulysses. America must be content with an illiterate lad. He expresses our germinal past. He expresses the movement of the American soul through all the sultry climaxes of the Nineteenth Century.

The Mississippi with its countless squalid towns and its palatial steamboats was a ferment of commingled and insoluble life. All the elements of the American East and all the elements of Europe seethed here, in the hunt of wealth. A delirium of dreams and schemes and passions, out of which shaped our genius for invention and exploitation. The whole gamut of American beginnings ran with the river. And Huck along. One rises from the book, lost in the beat of a great rhythmic flow: the unceasing elemental march of a vast life, cutting a continent, feeding its soil. And upon the heaving surface of this Flood, a human child: ignorant, joyous and courageous. The American soul like a midge upon the tide of a world.

Mark Twain was fifty when this work appeared. The balance of his literary life, before and after, went mostly to the wastage of half-baked, half-believed, half-clownish labor. And underneath the gibes and antics of the professional jester, brooded the hatred and resentment of a tortured child. Mark Twain, in his conscious mind, shared his people's attitude of contempt for "art and spiritual matters"—shared their standards of success. Mark Twain strove to make money and to please! This great soul came to New York and felt ashamed before the little dancing-masters of the magazines; felt humble before Richard Watson Gilder and William Dean Howells! Shared their conviction that he was only a crude, funny writer from Missouri; changed the texts of his books to suit their fancy. Mark Twain did not believe in his soul, and his soul suffered. Mark Twain believed, with his fellows, that the great sin was to be unpopular and poor, and his soul died. His one great work was the result of a burst of spirit over the dikes of social inhibition and intellectual fear. *Leaves of Grass* came in consequence of a similar bursting of the floodgates. American expression has ever had to break through the bars of pioneer conviction. But in the case of Whitman, the spirit remained free.

I recall vividly the one time I ever saw Mark Twain. There was a Benefit Performance for some Association for the Blind, in the ball-room of a New York hotel. My father took me. The platform was filled with blind men and women; silent faces that had somehow won serenity from their deprivation above the turmoil of those who saw. Joseph H. Choate was the chairman. My father told me that he was our Ambassador to England, and that he was the leader of the American Bar. I remember my vague and unresolved discomfort, looking at Mr. Choate. He had a bland and empty face. The face of a gigantic child. His well-groomed body curved with gracious gestures. It also was child-like, sweet, untrammeled. No passion seemed to have ruffled this great man: no harsh experience stamped him. He seemed to me the symbol of respectable vapidity. I did not realize that he was rather more the symbol of a world which barred experience—the true Ambassador of the pioneer.

Mr. Choate arose and spoke solemn, touching words. Speaking, his face wrinkled with complacence. A blind man was led to the piano: he played. A blind woman sang. And then, a tall spare person, natively grace-ful, naïvely timid, swung forward from his place among the blind. A vast shock of white hair fell from the clear forehead. Mark Twain! He opened his mouth. He hesitated. The long, nasal twang of the lower Mid-dle-West came with his words. Mark Twain—the hu-morist—America's funny man! His words were diffi-dent and sad. But everybody laughed. Mark Twain drew back. Turning half about, he seemed to take some heartening he needed from the unseeing eyes, from the wan smiles behind him. He began again. Mark

Twain's Western twang. The ball-room laughed once more. . . . For five minutes, the sad soul struggled with this reality about him—this reality that would laugh. His face was strained: his body seemed loose and nervous: his transparent voice withdrew gradually from the obtuse glee of his hearers. And then, Mark Twain gave up. He relaxed. He launched into an anecdote. The audience settled back, wreathed in smiles that somehow suggested to me the folds of an obese body. And Mark Twain rambled on. His jokes came slow and listless. He stood there almost still, with his back to the rows of them who could not see, and dropped the ungainly humor from his mouth. And the audience before him snouted it, guzzled it, roared with delight. At last, Mark Twain stopped. He fell back from the high applause to his seat and was out of sight among the sightless.

I remember how at that time I hated this noble-look-ing fool. It seemed to me that all the shallowpates I knew called Mark Twain their favorite author, bored me with quotations from his books. I hated Mark Twain because of them who seemed to love him. Now, I love him, because I faintly understand what a cross such love must have bound upon his back.

Mark Twain went through life, lost in a bitter blind-ness that is far more terrible than the hate of men like Schopenhauer or Jonathan Swift. The mighty pes-simists were fertile: they plowed great fields with their wrath and sowed them with their love. Mark Twain's was the misery of a love too feeble to create. In his later days, he wrote a book entitled *What is*

Man? It is the confession of his despondency, and its elucidation. It is the profane utterance of a defeated soul bent upon degrading the world to the low level where it was forced to live, whence came its ruin. An Old Man, in wooden dialogue, proves to a Young Man the folly of all human aspiration: proves to him that man is a machine:

YOUNG MAN: Do you believe in the doctrine that man is equipped with an intuitive perception of good and evil?

OLD MAN: Adam hadn't it.

YOUNG MAN: But has man acquired it since?

OLD MAN: No: I think he has no intuition of any kind. He gets all his ideas, all his impressions from the outside.

—The *reductio ad absurdum* of extraversion. And in the mouth of a man who by every inner circumstance and gift was an intuitive giant, belonged to the number of great artists! But Mark Twain knew that this was not the sort of book that his American readers wanted. So out of deference to their taste, or lack of confidence in his own, he hid it among his papers, where it was discovered at his death.* Until the end, he held forward to the public gaze the painted and powdered visage of a clown. †

* A carefully concealed edition of 250 copies, copyrighted in the name of J. W. Bothwell, the superintendent of the De Vinne Press, was printed privately and anonymously in 1906; and distributed among friends.

† Another of his works which he preferred to hide until his death was *The Mysterious Stranger,* a work which likewise expresses Mark Twain's arid and misanthropic view of life. When he was

The clown tragedy of Mark Twain is prelude to the American drama. The generic Clemens was a tender and dreaming and avid spirit, in love with beauty, in love with love. But he was born in the ranks of a hurling and sweating army. He forced himself to move with it at its own pace. He forced himself to take on its measures of success: to take on that distrust of life and love which so well defended the principal business of its march. For this betrayal of his soul, his soul brought him bitterness, and the mass of his works are failures.

. . . .

Mark Twain was a giant. Or a giant he would have grown to be, had he been nurtured at his nation's breast. But the centrifugal force was overwhelming. Mark Twain was flung away in outer darkness: where he did not belong, and where only lesser men adapt themselves to live. If we look for Miracle upon these Western plains, we must seek elsewhere.

The pioneering force increased, feeding upon itself. It meant febrile effort: the unending outplay of nerves, the atrophy of the restraining inner powers of reserve. Above all, it meant the Machine.

The channel of energy which led to America led to steam and the new uses of metal. Energy poured to the surfaces of life. The machine is simply an appendage to the human body. The normally balanced man

dead, this withering satire was brought out in a gay edition with gay-colored pictures and sold as a romance for holidays and children. The bitter genius of Jonathan Swift had no invention so sardonic as the fate which turned his *Gulliver's Travels* into a book for children. Here was the same irony at work once more.

had hands and feet of flesh. The extraverted man had hands and feet of iron. With swift logic, the machine became the god of the American world—both had a common parentage in Europe. And with equal logic, the machine took over the lands of the pioneer to be its chief domain. The vicious circle was rounded. For if the machine is the fresh product of the outpouring human soul, it soon became its master, and the soul that made it could not cease to feed it. Thus the new external world—the industrial world which America had created now drove the American out into an endless exteriorization. A sucking monster, which as it sucked swelled larger and so sucked more. Feed the machine of life. Do not stop. Open your veins!

Industrialism swept the American land and made it rich. Broke in on the American soul and made it poor. Our villages and cities were soon full of the maimed and the destroyed. A sagging, uncreative world bore witness to the fate of human spirit in a civilization which could persist alone by the denial of experience, by the mechanization of Desire.

For Desire would not be denied. It sickened and shriveled and grew perverse. It sought expression in neurotic arts, in obversely sensual religions, in sadistic interference with Desire in others: in all those twists of mental life that made a pat observer like Mr. Chesterton consider us aged and decrepit. But it *went on*. For it *is* life. And in the birth of each new generation, each new individual, it began once more its healthy journey, strong and fertile and inspired—until the accumulated might of environment and "education" turned it aside.

Do we realize how terrible in its perfection was the symbol of the Civil War?

The United States was from the outset an experiment in commercial politics. Massachusetts and Virginia had crystallized: they had formed their social institutions upon those *summa bona* of the pioneer—security of enterprise, freedom from philosophical or spiritual agitation, consecration to the ideals and criticism of material progress. And in their hour of success—before the influx of new human and economic elements upset their hold—they gave birth to a generation of mighty men. The contemporaries and successors of Washington and Hamilton and Jefferson were figures of decided intellectual dignity. They were products of a static stage, products of a brief rest from actual pioneering during which a morale could crystallize. But now, the frontier went westering once more. Strange European bloods turmoiled America. And the great Fathers disappeared. . . . Our land entered a period of hideous chaos which it is hard for us to-day to picture.

American wealth became fodder in a sty to be gorged and guzzled by stampeding pigs. The dignified commercial standards of New England were debased. Democracy became the cry of "Every one for himself." The best brains of the country went to the scramble for wealth. Politics fell into the hands of mediocre, often dishonest men who were debased by the venality of the rich and made arrogant by the new manipulated

46

power of the enfranchised masses.   Listen to Walt
Whitman's words about a typical Convention of the
sort which chose the nominees for President during
the period 1840 to 1860:

"The members who composed it were, seven-eighths of
them, the meanest kind of brawling and blowing office-hold-
ers, office-seekers, pimps, malignants, conspirators, mur-
derers, fancy-men, customhouse clerks, contractors, kept-
editors, spaniels well trained to carry and fetch, jobbers,
infidels, disunionists, terrorists, mail-riflers, slave-catchers,
pushers of slavery, creatures of the President, creatures of
would-be Presidents, spies, bribers, compromisers, lobbyers,
spongers, ruined sports, expelled gamblers, policy back-
ers, monte dealers, duelists, carriers of concealed weapons,
deaf men, pimpled men, scarred inside with vile disease,
gaudy outside with gold chains made from the people's
money and harlots' money twisted together; crawling, ser-
pentine men, the lousy combings and born freedom-sellers
of the earth. And whence came they? From backyards
and bar-rooms; from out of the customhouses and mar-
alls' offices, postoffices and gambling hells; from the President's house, the jail, the station-house; from unnamed
by-places where devilish disunion was hatched at mid-
night; from political hearses and from the coffins inside,
and from the shrouds inside of the coffins; from the tu-
mors and abscesses of the land; from the skeletons and
skulls in the vaults of the federal alms-houses; and from
the running sores of the great cities. Such, I say, form'd,
or absolutely control'd the forming of, the entire person-
nel, the atmosphere, nutriment and chyle, of our munici-
pal, State, and National politics—substantially permeating,
handling, deciding, and wielding everything—legislation,

nominations, elections, "public sentiment," etc., while the great masses of the people, farmers, mechanics, and traders, were helpless in their gripe. These conditions were mostly prevalent in the north and west, and especially in New York and Philadelphia cities; and the southern leaders (bad enough, but of a far higher order), struck hands and affiliated with, and used them." *

Slavery was merely the most ugly mark of the ugly spirit of the times. Abolition which had its home in Boston had its most treacherous foe in the same City. The commercial interests of the North encouraged slavery in the South, and turned with anger against the suggestion of its disappearance. Compromisers like Daniel Webster and Henry Clay, who covered the national sore with words, were the intellectual leaders of their day. All American life seemed hopelessly given up to anarchic self-aggrandizement. The South pushed for fresh fields: the North snuffled and turned against itself. Mexico was wantonly attacked, and robbed of a vast empire in the West. The South had singleness of purpose in its program of greedy domination. The more complex North had, to oppose it, conflicting greeds and in consequence a lack of purpose which goaded the South to arrogance and anger.

A black period indeed. The words of the Revolutionary Fathers had been fair. But in reality, they had conceived a State based on the sovereignty of secular wealth and dedicated to the safe business of its acquisition. And now, the well-ordered Combination

* *Origins of Attempted Secession.*

had broken out into a riot of self-seeking men. America was a welter of "mutually repellant particles." But the fair words of the Fathers were still heard. They spoke of "Perfect Union," "Justice," "the Blessings of Liberty," and "General Welfare." They were echoed in the daily papers. They were mouthed by politicians on public holidays. They were the American Myth. And among the many Americans who believed in them was one called Abraham Lincoln.

This morass was the world of Lincoln, the background of his political career. Lincoln was a frontiersman. In the backwoods of Kentucky and Illinois, where he lived his youth, the Pioneer conviction was untrammeled, the American Myth was undisputed. Lincoln was not intellectually aloof from his fellows and his time. He was no intellectual virtuoso. He believed in American institutions. He accepted Slavery as such a one, and did not permit the promptings of his heart to fling him into the heresy of Abolition. In our modern use, the radical is a man whose instincts force his mind to reject accustomed forms and to espouse new ones. In this sense, Lincoln was no radical at all. He had certain feelings about the evil of Slavery, about the logic of woman suffrage. But his convictions were at rest within the national laws and the national fact. Such a fact was Southern Slavery. But above all other facts, and fostering them, was the American Myth of "perfect union." For this greater fact, Lincoln was willing to wipe out lesser ones—and assuredly a lesser one, which he thought an evil one, like Slavery. But during all the years of his intellectual development, he was no rebel, he was no radical. A clean embodiment of the pioneer ideals: respectful of the rights of property—hence honest; faithful to the Constitution—hence loyal; a believer in the American Myths—hence an apt candidate for office at the hands of a sentimental electorate.

Listen to him in 1837:

"The heroes of the Revolution were pillars of the temple of liberty; and now that they have crumbled away, that temple must fall, unless we, their descendants, supply their places with other pillars, hewn from the solid rock of sober reason. Passion has helped us but can do so no more. It will in future be our enemy. Reason—cold, calculating reason—must furnish all the materials of our future support and defence." *

The stamp of pioneer intelligence is upon these words. They might have been uttered yesterday by any pragmatist—they might, that is, without the context of Lincoln's temperament. We know that Lincoln was in truth struggling against some restless being in himself: struggling to keep within the limits which his mind and his American training taught him were sound.

Moral and spiritual eminence has this about it, unlike mere intellectual supremacy: it does not isolate, it brings a vast capacity for being close to the ranks of men where intellectual genius must hold aloof. Lincoln could not have become our satisfying hero, had he had the sort of mind that distinguished Hamilton or

* From an address delivered before the Young Men's Lyceum in Springfield, Illinois.

Franklin. His mental average kept him close to the crude ore of the American world; kept him faithful to a Dream that seemed absurd enough during that saturnalia of disgusting disillusion; made it possible for him at last to achieve that "divine average" which is sung by his laureate, Walt Whitman.

For if we compare the training, utterance, behavior and conviction of this homely man during fifty years with the vision of him in the four years of his great service, one word comes to our minds: transfiguration. At the nadir of American materialism, American rationalism, this child of the pioneering plains became a saint.

He was the loyal child of this desolated world. He was dedicated to its practical idolatry. He was an apostle of its "Reason." And now, that world was foundering. Reduced to its lowest level, at last obedient to its implicit logic of destruction, it was rent asunder. And Lincoln who was the captain of its rescue is seen to move at the behest of impulse, motive, vision beyond its domain.

A materialistic world saved by a religious man. A practical union saved by a poet. A rational society saved by the abiding love of a mystic. Here at last our miracle.

If you do not believe that Lincoln was these things, read his letters, read his speeches. If you wish to gauge the miracle of his sainthood, think of the public who heard his words, think of his own earlier professions, think of the crude product of the American frontier whose words they were.

129996

The Civil War was a natural climax. Like all wars, it was stupid, an orgy of incompetence and dishonesty and greed. It raised into the places of power a few men who were able, great numbers who were not. It brought forth all the ugly passions of mankind, magnified follies and vices, warped virtues, enflamed judgments: it reduced the nation to the lowest social levels. An ordinary war. What glorified the man who carried it through?

Abraham Lincoln did not dominate in the manner of Washington or Wilson. He was not of the miserable Show. Rather he walked through it, with his own faith and love. In this way he was master. He often judged and ruled alone. He could be relentless. And yet, there was a difference. To come close to his personality is to be convinced that Lincoln's preëminence was due to a spiritual quality: is to be convinced that Lincoln's chief attention did not go to the mere end of beating the South, but always to the sacred means of preserving life upon a religious level throughout the bloody business. And this is Miracle indeed.

He was a practical man. His words and his official acts abound in canniness. But this very fact makes the more luminous that mystical sense of life—even of life in Wartime—*as an end in itself*, which was the true guide of his steps.

Without his penetrating mind, his grasp of material details, he could perhaps not have restored the Union. But without the religious saturation of his entire being, he could not have been what we mean by Lincoln. His place in the American heart emphatically does not come from what he did, but from what he was.

The accent of Lincoln's voice recalls the Hebrew singers. This is no accident. Nor is it to be explained by Lincoln's knowledge of the Bible. Every orator of his day knew the Bible as well as Lincoln. Edward Everett, Wendell Phillips knew it far better. No external or intellectual reason can explain why we turn instinctively from the divine words of this Westerner to the divine words of David or Isaiah. The truth is simpler. Lincoln had become full of a great vision, a vision far beyond even the broad business of War. It brought him serenity and ease. Words came pure from his prophetic faith as light comes up from fire. Words were the luminous uprising particles of his conviction.

He moved through a doubting, wrangling world and he alone kept the faith. His greatest trial was his own people. The intellectuals of Boston pitied and patronized him.* Wendell Phillips called him names. New

---

* The historian, Henry Adams (see Chapter VI), certainly one of the most astute and sensitive observers of the time, says this of himself fifty years later in *The Education of Henry Adams:* "Had young Adams been told that his life was to hang on the correctness of his estimate of the new President, he would have lost. He saw Mr. Lincoln but once: at the melancholy function called an Inaugural Ball. Of course he looked anxiously for a sign of character. He saw a long, awkward figure; a plain, ploughed face; a mind, absent in part, and in part evidently worried by white kid gloves; features that expressed neither self-satisfaction nor any other familiar Americanism, but rather the same painful sense of becoming educated and of needing education that tormented a private secretary; above all, a lack of apparent force. Any private secretary in the least fit for his business would have thought, as Adams did, that no man living needed so much education as the new President but that all the education he could get would not be enough."

53

York burned him in effigy. His generals and secretaries hoped to succeed him in office. The most passionate lovers of the Union fell into despond when they first caught sight of his huge, ungainly figure. And yet, he was *sure*. The "cold, calculating, unimpassioned Reason" he had extolled in 1837 could not have brought him to this certainty. Reason was in the camp of his enemies and doubters. The "reason" which had foundered the country was now prepared to prove by syllogistic means that Abe Lincoln was incapable of saving it. And yet, he could smile: and could keep his temper: and be sure.

Finally, his love went forth over the land, making true all those things which the *fact* of history denied. The treachery of those who should have held him up, the folly and ambition of the faithful, even the anger of the South came gradually within the spell of this man's love, and disappeared. A new nation imperceptibly received the balm of a new understanding.

America is not mature enough to know what is the nature of her wealth in Lincoln: has not yet realized why Lincoln fills that place in our hearts which reason peremptorily demands for that far abler man, George Washington. The keenest pioneer minds protest; Washington was a great military genius, a great political genius, a creator. For twenty years he mastered American life. Lincoln, thrust up by political accident from obscurity to fame, held the wheel nobly during four years of storm. He was a great man, a great conserver; but Washington was "the man who made us."

Unanswerable reasons. And yet, the Father of his Country grows dimmer in our love. And Lincoln, soon or late, enters the emotional life of all Americans, rich and poor, intelligent or average, good and bad. He is the perfect hero precisely for this cause: any American may find in him his own desire.

At bottom, Lincoln personifies the crude American myth. The early masters in our history were in great part aristocrats. Washington was the richest American of his time. Most of his fellows in control were gentlemen in the English sense—ran counter to the legend which themselves had sealed in the Declaration of Independence, that America was a land of equal opportunity. Any poor boy, spoke the myth, might become President. Other poor boys had, besides Lincoln —Andrew Jackson, Andrew Johnson—but he was the archetype. A little later the myth changed somewhat. Not "any poor boy might become President" expressed the heart of the wish, but "any poor boy might become a millionaire." Heroes are flexible. Lincoln who was poor remained the dazzling precedent. If he had not actually lived, America must have invented him.

Thus on the level of sheer material success, Lincoln answered a need and became a hero. To a more sophisticated group, equally obsessed with the sentimentality of wealth, Lincoln is dear because—as he himself believed—he saved the traditional halo of the Republic. A still active generation worships the Constitution. For them, the founders of the Union form an hagiography: the works of Hamilton and Jay and Marshall are sacred works. Charles Péguy would have

called this worship our *older mysticism*. It supplies
emotional support to our capitalist and legal oligar-
chies. They revere Lincoln because *he saved their
Church*. During sixty years American economic history was the grunting of hogs—under the mystic patronage of the Constitution. Then something broke.
The hogs stampeded. The trough was smashed. Lincoln put matters once more to rights: reconciled the
porkish factions: gave over the American lands once
more to industrial exploitation—peaceful piggishness.
"Blessed be the name of Lincoln."

But even in the lowest consciousness, the place of
Lincoln is something nobler, deeper, than any of these
reasons. Even in the lowest consciousness some sense
of the man's spiritual grandeur has eaten down—before
the corrupt mind looks for its practical interpretation.

Abraham Lincoln prophesies the break from the materialistic culture of pioneer America: personifies the
emergence from it of a poetic and religious experience
based on the reality of American life—and in terms
so simple that they have become the experience of all.
This is our true wealth in Lincoln.

He makes manifest our faith in the American's capacity for spiritual growth beyond the limits clamped
upon him by conditions—conditions physical, economic, temperamental. They forced American energy
away from the paths that lead to fulness and to beauty,
away from life. Conditions surely more obsessive than
have obtained in any other land, in any other time.
And now, in this black hour came a man who seemed
by training and by will to accept the darkness, to move

in unison with his benighted people—upon however
high a level. And a great crisis, that was bound to be,
arose and worked on this child of the pioneers. And
behold, he was transfigured! A bright spirit was born
in him. He became strong and beautiful. He became
articulate. Strength and beauty went forth from him
into his world.

.   .   .   .

To the blind eye of the historian, that strength and
beauty seemed to go forth only to their destruction.
Lincoln was surrounded by politicians, vindictive igno-
ramuses, New England pedants. Lincoln was mur-
dered. Greed and revenge took over the South and
beat it into an impotence from which it has not yet
recovered. The country lapsed into a new saturnalia
of material exploitation. Negro slavery was whipped.
Wage slavery was victor. A vast continent sagged into
self-indulgence. It was drunk on speculation, quite as
its politicians were drunk on words and whiskey. It
had no mind to suggest the conduits of its energy. It
seemed to react from Lincoln and the War, as an ugly
child reacts from a sermon and a lesson.* The Trail
of the pioneer hardened into the Railroad. Pioneering
became Industrialism. Industrialism became a tool,

---

* If the reader wants a raw picture of the nature of these men
and times, let him read *The Book of Daniel Drew*. Whatever
changes the editor, Bouck White, may have made in the illiterate
diaries of this Wall Street magnate, it is impossible that he should
have falsified the general tone and content of the volume. The
dualism of this man, who, on weekdays lied, stole, betrayed friends,
wrecked railroads, ruined thousands, and on Sundays founded
theological seminaries and went to church, might be incredible to
any one not understanding the American background.

not for production but for accumulation. Giants like Gould, Fiske, Rockefeller, Morgan, Harriman, with the consciousness and tactics of the Stone-age, expressed America. The old mysticism was dead. But where was the new? Where was the material that could take fire from Lincoln's flame?

We shall see how the perspective of to-day gives the historian his answer. The degraded years that lie between the present and the Civil War are gone. The railroads are built. The West is strewn with ugly towns. The years are gone, and the little men that filled them with their clamorous greed. Lincoln remains. But not as the emancipator of the slaves: not as the savior of a Union that has yet to prove it was worth saving. What lives in Lincoln is the miracle of his achievement of spiritual values from the crude life about him. What comes direct to us is the challenge of his premise: Such was the experience of this child of the pioneer, such then can also be the experience of us all.

II. NEW ENGLAND

The causes of Puritanism may be left to that still ideal scientist, the psychological historian. And he, when he exists, will tell you that all causes are inscrutable to man, and that in history as in mechanics we must be satisfied with sequence.

We have certain fairly consequential facts. We know that in the days when Shakespeare wove his gorgeous feudal fabrics, there was already rife in England a tendency toward the homeliest of homespun. Privilege was brocaded: also, Privilege was churched. A disfranchised Middle-class was grumbling, who wanted Privilege but were hopelessly excluded from Brocade. Church and State controlled in feudal splendor. A lowly but potential class who desired power moved first to dissociate power from the finery they could not share. The Puritan attack was upon the outposts of Authority: was upon the sanctity of wealth and the luxuriance of ritual in which Authority was dressed.

The earliest Puritans did not dream of separation from the English Church; they wanted to capture that Church. Nor of separation from the English soil. They hoped to have their share of it. They recognized that the prestige of the English Church and the security and wealth of the ruling caste were one. They saw this security and wealth expressed in the Church rituals. They disagreed with these rituals, with the manner of life that the ruling caste defended, because they disagreed with the assumption of power that was thus symbolized in the minds of the English people. Against this assumption, they pitted their doctrines of moral and ritual austerity. But these characters—commonly known as Puritan—were at the beginning the negative side of the Puritan intention. Their positive demand was power.

The established classes felt the true thrust in the Puritan assault. A restless and virile part of England's people were in reality assailing the Realm's Masters. Their attack was upon the masters' ways of life and worship. The retaliation came on the same level.

The issue could have been joined upon no other. Social consciousness was a feeble growth in the Seventeenth Century. No stand could have been made directly upon it. But religious consciousness was long since mature. A social movement could not hope to enlist the emotions of the masses, save it moved in the religious plane. The duel between English noble and English yeoman was possible alone on the dogmatic platform where the Puritans unconsciously but unerringly had staged it.

The ideal democracy of God had survived the Renaissance. In England, at least, it was already feeding the impulse toward the practical democracy of man. Since, however, ritual was the chosen terrain for the social struggle, questions of ritual of course became endowed with the emotional content of the true battle underneath. Community of ritual represented commu-

nity of life. Difference of ritual was the sign of mortal
enmity. Before the Century was done, the class struggle had burst through its religious cloak. Persecution
led down to civil war. But for the present, all of the
latent passion of civil war still pressed upward into
terms of dogmatic difference. And if these quarrels
had the force to thrust new life upon a continent three
thousand miles away, it was because there moved within
them the energy of Cromwell, the energy that dealt
death to Feudalism, and that has spread the hegemony
of the Middle-class throughout the world.

But why the most virulent and significant form of
this vast upheaval became Puritan among the Anglo-
Saxons, is a mystery of cause that lies beyond us.

What follows has the voluptuous exactness of simple logic.

The first Puritans landed at Plymouth in 1620. Persecution had driven them, thirteen years before, from
their town in Yorkshire. They had joined earlier English separatists in Leyden. But it was not long before
Holland irked. Their children were beginning to speak
Dutch and to behave like Dutchmen. Their identity
was threatened—not religiously but socially. They
had no wish to be merged into the material world of
a little Republic which they actually despised for the
religious toleration that had made possible their coming. Passion for power had not inclined them to leave
England for so small an end. They preferred the virgin mystery of Massachusetts.

By this time, however, their separatist life, the mold
of persecution had fairly formed what henceforth would

be known as the Puritan disposition. The will-to-power, intensified by the need of compensation for an adverse place in the world, was at its heart. This will had led to open conflict upon the one conscious social plane of the Seventeenth Century: religion. The importance the Puritans attached to ritual was therefore simply the importance they attached to themselves. The loathing in which they held all ritual disagreement was simply their unchristian but altogether human feeling for their foes: a thousand times enhanced, since they were sure that God was on their side.

Separatism had brought with it in England a vigilant menace. Death or confiscation of property was just the sort of persuasion to drive the Puritan headlong in his chosen way, make him a fanatic. We have seen that this direction led toward austerity of ritual, purity of conduct—all the compensatory reactions to a party that was given up to voluptuous and rounded living. But now that these Puritans were in Holland, where for a while the pressure was removed, the direction did not change. Perhaps, a permanent life in the Netherlands might have abolished Puritanism. But their brief sojourn in a foreign land from which they were eager to keep themselves apart merely increased the Puritan disposition. And when they were at last on a continent of their own, there came other reasons for the continuance of this deep-grained attitude toward sensuous living. Even if England had ceased to threaten them from afar, even if Archbishop Laud had not kept the antagonism hot, the Puritan ways of life must have gone on and sharpened in America.

For on this savage continent, those ways were justi-
fied, were rendered even marvelously right by *facts*.
We know that asceticism has its roots in the same senses
that are gratified by indulgence. Pain, like pleasure,
we know to be a function of Desire. The man who
denies the flesh is brother to him who is its slave. But
if the ferocity of Puritan denial is an obverse form of
sensuality, it has vast advantages over the conduct of
high living. It conserves energy: it sharpens wits: it
quickens all the machinery of action. In other words,
it prepares the Pioneer.

The Puritan had begun by desiring power in England. This desire had turned him deviously into austere ways. He had soon learned the sweets of austerity. Now he became aware of the power over himself,
over others, over physical conditions which the austere
life brought with it. A virgin and hostile continent demanded whatever energy he could bring to bear upon
it. A frugal, self-denying life released that energy far
better than could another.

Let the reader recollect what we have already seen
in the first chapter to be the general character of the
pioneer. Pioneer and Puritan met on a base of psychological and temperamental unity. They merged and
became one. The Puritan's nature fitted him superbly
to be a pioneer. The pioneer existence made permanent
the Puritan's nature.

It was not long before a dozen little theocracies dot-
ted the coast of Massachusetts. Intolerance was the
creed of these communities. Matters of ritual, which
had served as standards of English social conflict, be-

came here the standards of social and economic soli-
darity: war measures of the New Englander against
the menacing American hinterland. But if devotion to
self-denial and its consequent efficiency was deep in the
Puritan soul, so was its appetite for schism. Ferocious
ritual arguments began anew in Salem, Newtown, Boston. And new dissenters were flung off. Rhode Island
and Connecticut were soon peopled with Puritan con-
gregations which had not found Massachusetts pure
enough in dogma and in life. But at the end, the recur-
rent menace of the Mother country—now religious, now
economic—annealed the warring groups. New England
became a prosperous fact. Already, New England was
far more.

Spaniard and Frenchman and English Catholic had
also set up colonies in North America: had forced
themselves to become pioneers. Alone the Puritan in
his adjustment to pioneer conditions needed no great
psychological conversion. Each other emigrant had
sailed to our shores, bearing with him the culture, the
religion, the habits of sense and mind of a Mother
country. The rude demands of the frontier compelled
him to throw off his culture, reform his mental habits,
convert his energy. A painful and imperfect process.
But the Puritan had done all these things before he
came! He had denied the English culture, swung to
the farther pole from the rich expression that was
Shakespeare: he had denied his Church: he had denied
all of the inner English life that was stored up in the
forms and manners of the English realm. His dissent-

ing way and the dissenting way of the pioneer were already one before he went upon it.

In this difference of temperamental fitness may be read the doom that came upon New France, New Holland and New Spain—may be read the triumph of New England. In it, indeed, may be read the comparative Latin failure in modern times at colonizing, the great achievement of the British. English energy is centrifugal. Comfort, home-ties are weak against their outward flowing will-to-power. All the Anglo-Saxons, less than their neighbors, needed a complete conversion to become life-denying, culture-denying pioneers. The Anglicans of Maryland and Virginia were more liberal at first, and the climate of the South was warmer. But the stress of America soon induced them into channels very near to the Puritan direction. After all, they were all Anglo-Saxons, they were brothers. The soul oppression and asceticism of New England they did not immediately share. Their wills went more directly forth into the world. They built upon Slavery a feudal state of social and industrial oppression so intense and complete that it required four years of civil war to break it up. But the feudality of the South was quite as materialistic, as unluminous as the theodicy of the North. Southern energy simply responded to the American call without the initial inner discipline by which the Puritan perfected his response. Gaming and hunting took the place of endurance-prayers. Lust for material accumulation was unleashed without the primary Puritan stage of grace-accumulation. But both North and South shared the rationale of contempt for the "softer" activities of life, the same absorption in the business of making money. Their methods were so far apart that finally they clashed in civil war. Their goal was one.

Money is the symbol of projected power: of power within the outer world. Money assumed a sanctity in America beyond the dream of Europe. Both Puritan and Cavalier were conquerors. They sensed the sweets of conquest every time they cleared a forest or bridged a river or swindled Indians. But in the Puritan, the primary repressive impulse had built up a philosophy for the new way of life. The Southern Anglo-Saxon, less repressed, more openly in touch with the objective world, became a politician. But he could not rival the intellectual leadership—the more perfect fitness—of New England.

So gradually, the English colonies on the Atlantic seaboard crowded out the Spanish, Dutch and French. And New England by virtue of its inherent preparation became the *mind*, though not necessarily the motor, of the new English world.

The will-to-power and the religious impulse are not always opposed. In the pioneer they were. And the Puritan became a pioneer. He spoke about Creed: he meant dominion. He thought it was because of God that he left England: but what he found across the sea was Empire.

Religion as a revealed, mystical consciousness—the religion of Christ—was among the weakening realities which the Puritan discarded when he set sail from England. The ancient might of Christianity lay in the

Form it brought to life as a unified experience in God. In this sense, Europe had long been Christian. But this sense could live only in men whose inner energy was great, in whom the subjective life held dominion over the outer world. This sense was doomed when energy went forth upon the frenzied material career which dated from the Renaissance, and at length flung man upon the spiritual desert of the Twentieth Century. Luther is less the symbol of the decline of Christianity as a world-force, than Columbus. Columbus made for energy a channel into a boundless outer world. The boundless inner world of Christ was shrunken by his passage: and Christ withered. The Puritan movement was simply a chapter in the long history of religious decadence. And in this function, it stands revealed. It was essentially an irreligious force: it was in practice a component of pioneering.

The soil of Europe was still rich with its spiritual past. Not so America. The spiritual fall was slow in Europe. In America, it was immensely swift. Absorption in the outer world became with us an imperious need: compelled attention to impersonal channels. The personal life faded. The personal God also.

. . . .

Meantime, however, New England settled down into a true community. By 1640, with the Puritan ascendency in England, the great emigration ceased. Even without the influx from across the sea, the population of the colonies doubled every quarter-century. A period of comparative rest set in: and with it, the beginnings of a native culture.

The Puritan became a manufacturer, a merchant and a shipper. He became prosperous and independent. His financial and commercial interests were never separate from his Church: the theocracy had seen to that. Soon, these interests commanded—and commanded the Church also. Material affairs colored and embraced the entire life of the thriving colonies.

No religious tenet ran counter to this natural consummation. Was not Moralism an aid to commerce? With it came thrift, sobriety, a level head. With it came the dominion of those who were moral, over those who were not. By the same token, education served the commercial powers. The young, under discipline of their religion, were hardened and whittled down into prime tools for Property. Thus grew the material culture of the Puritan which was to become the culture of the United States.

Harvard and the other quasi-sectarian universities became the founts of its peculiar and thorough inspiration. The sanctity of earning, the security of that which had been earned, the blessedness of knowledge which sharpened wits and the futility of all experience which was not *instrumental* soon merged into an harmonious attitude. Materialism was an invisible Magnet toward which each element of New England thought and life needed to point. The cultured spoke of law and learning, of faith and good and God. But though these were the fair words they used, the trend of each of these matters—its specific gravity—was determined by the Magnet. And all else—all that did not *point*— did not exist. Thus, Henry Adams, writing of the period before the Civil War: "In essentials like religion, ethics, philosophy: in history, literature, art: in the concepts of all science except perhaps mathematics, the American boy stood nearer the year One than the year 1900." Doubtless. . . . And yet, New England had its own magnetized expression for all these matters. And such harmony is culture of a sort.

The desire for that completed consciousness which we call spiritual did not die, even in New England. Neither spirit nor beauty. They simply fled from the magnetized reality. They became *transcendental.*

We have seen a genius like Mark Twain stifled beneath the brutal burden of the pioneering West. Here now is a victim of a different sort: the sensitive and aspiring scholar, beating his wings above the obtuse fields of his New England: Ralph Waldo Emerson. Surely, like Mark Twain, a subject worthy the attention of the gods who prize the failures of the human spirit, crushing perhaps some subtle wine from them as men crush grapes.

Emerson had the equipment of a true cultural leader. He had vision, he had considerable mental power, he had the genius of aspiration. And yet his books are vague, his instances remote. The colors of his words brush off like the dust on a moth's wing. The true *motif* of Emerson is an hysterical plea: his works are essentially discards from weakness.

The Soul, Beauty, Communion with Nature which is God, *are* possible, he seems to say with just this emphasis. And in the locus where he hopes to find them, he stands revealed. For Emerson's first gesture is the withdrawal of defeat. Implicitly, he leaves the world —the actual world of men, New England's world—to the low enemy. "Beauty and Spirit are lonely fellows," he seems to shrill. "Come with me and I will show them to you. For they are not within the homes of men. They are far away. And only in secluded spots where men's feet have not approached, can you find earthly portals to them."

Thomas Carlyle ventured the regret, in praising his friend's book, that he had not applied such spiritual vehemence to the reality of life. But Emerson did not understand: he was so far afield that he no longer seemed to know of a reality he had neglected. To him, the world not alone of enterprise but even of passion and of thought—the world *he* knew—was so wholly measured by materialistic standards, that it did not occur to him to find his haven save in the air: place his "over-soul" among the stars. To him, the gesture of human aspiration was a transcending leap away from all that was mortal-human.

Here is a little sentence that bares his tragedy. He speaks of the Poet. "The details, the prose of nature he must omit, and give us only the spirit and the splendor." We know what the details and prose of Emerson's New England were. A community rigid in the purposes of acquisition, intolerant of pause, derisive of the silences of life: a world reduced to the low simplicities of profit under the foot of whose one dynamic impulse there could grow only the toughest weeds: a New England of ugly housings, futile decorations, buried pleasures. From this sere stuff Emerson could

distil no essence for his thirst. He and his followers
starved on the crass food about them: their stomachs
spewed it up. So they concocted air-brews for substitutes. They could not face the truth that the "spirit
and the splendor" they desired were to be found alone
in the "details and prose" which they rejected. And to
be found nowhere else.

"I will make the poems of materials, for I think they are
        to be the most spiritual poems;
And I will make the poems of my body and of mortality,
For I think I shall then supply myself with the poems of
        my Soul, and of immortality."

—Thus Walt Whitman. The difference between
strength and weakness: between the mystic whose Mystery is consciousness of All, and the mystic whose Mystery is escape. . . .

It would be hard to overstate the place of Emerson
and of his school in American intellectual life. For
two generations during which Whitman was ignored
and Thoreau wrongly relegated to the place of Emersonian disciple, the Sage of Concord ruled supreme in
thoughtful circles. His philosophy supplied a norm
for our poetry and fiction, his manner became the manners of the cultured. An ironic tragedy, indeed. Emerson, who abhorred American affairs and was so re-
pugned by the traffic of reality that he could only with
reluctance declare himself in favor of freeing slaves,
was delivered up into the patronage of the material
world he hated: and did his share of feeding it, easing
it, giving it strength.

The paradox soon disappears. Æsthetic and spiritual values impose a discipline on man only when they are mined from the crude ore of his existence: when they partake of the consciousness of the Whole. Such values saturated Athens, lifted the mediæval mind to its practical Gothic grandeurs. But the Over-soul of Emerson gave to a material American world the very dualism it required. For the American also demanded his "poetry," his "spiritual pursuits." Even the rapt devotion of a pioneering continent left some energy unchanneled that yearned for non-material affairs. But any sort of spiritual values that invaded the Bank, contested dominion of the Earth, must have proved irksome to the pioneer. Moreover, running undirected, such energy might cause criticism, disaffection, might weaken materialism's hold. Unwittingly, tragically, the good Ralph Waldo Emerson solved the problem for his foes.* Behold! here was a path to "poetry and spirit" so splendidly remote from crass reality that it could in no way lead to it. If the pursuit of beauty took one to these chill Emersonian heavens, why then of course the earth was safe for the pursuit of money. Here was Emerson and his school scooping the vagrant

---

* There is of course criticism—social and realistic criticism—in Emerson's writings. At times, even, there is the statement of his awareness of the importance of American scenes to the American poet and artist. But the effect of a man's message depends upon the density and temperament of his work, not upon the subject-matter of desultory paragraphs. Emerson might protest "that our Banks and tariffs, the newspapers and caucus . . . rest on the same foundations of wonder as the Town of Troy." His own aloof absorption was far more impressive. And *it* impressed.

energy away, flinging it on high in the region of the Sun, where it could do no harm!

So it came about that Emerson supplied the needed philosophic decoration for the seats of learning where men were prepared for the Business of life: and for the drawing-rooms and lecture-halls where men and women, returning from the Business, relaxed. And when the New England culture wreathed its dominion over the land, the transcendentalists floated along, with their sweet words blessing the harsh hold of Puritan and pioneer upon the younger generations.

The timid and unhearty eked out other avenues of escape from the dread vehemence of American life. The most famous way was that of Edgar Allan Poe. The exoticism of Poe is quite as American as the transcendentalism of Emerson and Hawthorne. But it is far less significant. We observe to-day in his work, the makeshift of an imagination that had no world to dwell in. In his rejection of experience and of America as a place to dream in, we recognize the transposed gesture of the pioneer. Poe, as a matter of fact, was far more *transcendental* than Emerson whom he was pleased to call a "ninny." He made his escape by another channel and landed in a macabre region of synthetic horrors.

Poe is the most famous of the American artists whose imagination could not reside in the American world. Henry James heads the lengthening lists of those who had to escape even with their bodies.*

* James McNeil Whistler seems to have combined the methods of Poe and Henry James.

James is one of those artists of small vitality in whom the vitality they have—by economy of life and conduct—is expended in the weaving of intricate designs. Contemporary with Vittoria and Palestrina, the Roman Church had many such composers: past masters of counterpoint whose works even to-day are patterns of technique and are, yet, altogether dead. Henry James, by accident of birth, was in a material position to escape the struggle of American life. When a Frenchman goes to Tahiti he is still part of France. The thousand-year-old roots are long enough to span the seas. But the American is a recent planting. Uproot him, and he may lose the tentative beginning of American life which is all that America so far can give him. This lack is clear in James: this lack of roots. He was a strange sort of monster—to my prejudiced eye—with vast peripheral development and no depths. A sort of inverted Octopus. His intricate designs strike me as shallow, his characters as flat films upon which glance kaleidoscopic colors. All his life he gave up to the creation of a world rootless like himself, brilliant and intricate and superficial like his own centrifugal life. In the sense that art is the expression of clever and idle fingers, his work is impeccable in form. But in the sense that art is the register upon a deep human consciousness of dimensioned and dynamic life, his novels are formless.

The influence of Poe has been restricted to literary episodes, largely abroad where his clear technique and his dim personality were profitably taken up by the refugees from the growing Industrial disorder, and made into an example and a legend. The heart of the method of Henry James for escaping the urgent density of our world requires the means to live in Europe. A few *émigrés* are vociferous and dull in London where James was quiet and sweet-voiced. The magazines that cater to secluded ladies have many pages in which the faults of these two masters are discreetly aped. But the Emersonian escape alone has become a part and tool of the American point of view.

Emerson supplied the dualism which our material obsession needed to survive. The hypocrisy of the American who goes to church on Sunday and bleeds his brother Monday, who leads a sexually vicious life and insists on "pure" books, draped statues and streets cleared of prostitutes, who preaches liberty and democracy and free-speech, and supports the subtlest Oligarchy of modern times, found support by a bitter irony in the books of this pure spirit.

. . . .

And then the hegemony of New England.

We have seen the practical convergence of Puritan and pioneer. The Puritan lands had settled. From their ways and from their problems, they construed a culture. Puritanism was at last articulate. It could therefore serve throughout America as the rationale for pioneering. America was a nation of frontiers. New England only could supply a complete philosophy to meet its needs. In its moralities, its gospels, its seats of learning, its cultural decorations, New England fitted.

Had New England stayed at home, its word must

have gone abroad no less. But the hegemony of New England as intellectual and social leader was now advanced by its dispersion as a community. The Protestant tendency of indefinite splitting-up into highly antagonistic creeds by no means lessened with the Nineteenth Century. The new sects were legion. Each of them thrust out from the New England home, and sought a home of its own in the inviting West. And each, under whatever guise, under whatever protest of differentiation, carried with it the essentials of New England culture.* What is more, the New England farmer became restless on purely economic grounds. His rocky soil which he had never learned to cultivate with the love of the mellowing peasant, began to fail him. He left it, and pushed for the more open West. And wherever the New Englander went,—Ohio, Nebraska, Utah, California—New England went along. The Puritan voice alone was clear. The Puritan vision alone was true. The Puritan books alone were

---

* This holds good with the polygamous *Mormons* quite as with the *Shakers,* who did not marry at all. It is impossible here to go into the nature and bases of Mormonism. It was a sexual revolt from the surrounding repression, that took along with it on its harried journey West all of the other Puritan prohibitions and ideals. The new Bible, *The Book of Mormon,* where the whole concept of the chosen people and of the new revelation of Christ is transferred to America and to American history, marks the Mormons' will-to-power. Suffice it, here, to say that once comfortable in Utah, their religious impulse faded. The Mormons soon became a prosperous commercial and political clique, more like New England than New England, and in control of the resources of a vast State. Quite properly, the house in Salt Lake City which holds the offices of the leaders of the Church has the exact appearance of a New York bank building.

read. An adumbrating world looked to Boston as to
the source of knowledge.

A new generation sprang from the American soil:
away from the frontier, released from the pioneering
rhythm. New old races crossed the seas, and America
was a Babel of tongues. But these tongues were stilled
before the clear articulation of New England. New
England's voice was everywhere: in the colleges of Illinois, in the journals of Kansas, in the churches of
Montana, in the statutes of Oklahoma. Boston had
become an Italian and Irish city. Connecticut and
Massachusetts were Catholic states in which the Puritan universities of Yale and Harvard stood alone like
arid rocks above a turbid sea. Even the name Puritan
was gone from the usages of men. But throughout
America, in the seats of power and in the seats of utterance, the Puritan was master.

III. THE CHOSEN PEOPLE

THE early Puritans came to Massachusetts in the faith that they were the Chosen People. In this faith, they founded their miniature theodicies after the stern manner of the Old Testament. In it, they looked with condescension, often with contempt, upon their neighbors. They were sure that Christ, in his second coming, would snub Europe and land in Boston.

Two centuries passed. New England was breaking up and scattering Westward. Jesus had not arrived. But now another Chosen People, of the race of Jesus, came instead. To-day, more than three million of Jews live in the United States. One million and a half—one quarter of its entire population—live in the city of New York.

The kinship of the Puritan and Jew, as they appear on the American scene, is close. There was no fortuity in the New Englander's obsession with the Hebrew texts, in his quite conscious taking on of the rôle of Israel in a hostile world. Like the Jew, the Puritan was obsessed with the dream of power: elected a career of separatism from the world in order to attain it: took to himself a personal and exacting God in order to justify it: traversed the seas in order to effect it. And as with the Puritan, so with the Jew, once free in a vast country, the urge of power swiftly shook off its religious and pietistic way, and drove untrammeled to material aggression. In their intense and isolated will, the Puritan and Jew were kin. Also, in their function as American pioneers. But one must not press the relationship too far. As occurs so often upon the theater of the world, channels of energy, though flung from widely different sources and tending to diverse points, for a season flowed together and fertilized one field. No more. . . .

There is a Jewish paradox, and this paradox is perhaps the equation of the Jew's survival, of his immense success. Always, he has been moved by these seemingly antagonistic motives: the will-to-power, the need of mystical abnegation, the desire for comfort on the sensuous and mental planes. When these impulses converged and created a resultant philosophy of life, the Jew has functioned. Otherwise not.

In ancient Hebrew times, these forces brought about Jehovah. Jahveh remained a tribal, a proprietory God. As such, he was the true master over Israel. "He has commanded unto each people its ruler. . . . And he has elected Israel for his own portion: he nourishes it in his discipline like a first born." * A stern and jealous father, functioning fully in the Jewish need of self-humiliation. But behold the other force of the Jewish nature making this God the one God, the Lord over all. No more grandiose satisfaction for the Jew's will-to-power could have been imagined. The little tribe at once set itself over the world. Its Lord was the Lord of hosts, and its rôle in human history became

* *Jesus, Son of Sirach* (Apocr.): XVIII, 14–15.

divine. Yet, with this satisfaction of the lust for dominance, the equal thirst for suffering, for immolation is not neglected.

In the Dispersion, the equation did not fundamentally change. The Jews were scattered and were suffering. Even the little kingdom was no more, which their genius had lifted up—to their own contentment—above the kingdoms of earth. It became needful, merely, to stress the spiritual part of their syllogism of power and mystical debasement. The belief in Israel's universal Priesthood was an ample response to the most abject reality. Jewish pride, Jewish mysticism, Jewish masochism met on a sublimated plane. To it, the Jew was able, in every trial, to rise up and find the solace of his Reason, the satisfaction of his senses. So he survived. The stiff-necked Jew was actually the most flexible man that the world had ever known. He needed power, comfort, the sense of being lost in a greater Whole. Inordinate needs, and yet, above his brethren, he was able to attain them. He had the genius for *transferring* them, when they encountered obstacles in life, to some other but still *real* plane. And I say *real,* because the Jew never lost the objective balance, never leaped up in the transcendental escape. The plane to which he lifted his needs was ever one upon which his emotions, instincts, experience and activity of life could remain in play. If he was persecuted and despised, he found his sense of power in his religious mission. If he was forced to live in an evil Ghetto, physically tortured, he found his comfort in the joys of suffering and denial. If he was rich and great in the world, his synagogue brought him back to the sweet misery of mystical humiliation.

With modern times, Talmudic Judaism could no longer serve as a complete expression of the Jewish will. Scientific inquiry, the rational method instituted by Descartes, were conquering the world. The immemorial paradox of the Jew needed a modern means. No more perfect paradigm of his adaptability could be conceived than the rational mysticism of Spinoza. It is one of those rare expressions of personality, in which the genius of an entire people culminates and lives. The Book of Isaiah is not more Jewish than the *Ethica Ordine Geometrico Demonstrata.*

In Spinoza, the Jewish paradox comes to this: God is infinite, and man is lost in Him, yet God must be contained within the consciousness of man. The first clause satisfies the need of abnegation, the second the need of power. Spinoza responds by *rationally* proving the infinity and the inscrutability of God. Since the reason is a function of man, and since by this function God has been ascertained, God in all His attributes comes within human reach. God is non-anthropomorphic. Yet he is in man's power, since man's mind proves him. He is universal, yet finite mind encompasses His being. All substance, including man, is a part of God. There is thus no true distinction between finite and infinite. And if man, who is finite, knows an infinite world, he is infinite as well. He loses his identity, disappears from the snug center of the universe he had for so long occupied. But he reappears in a far more powerful modification: as an inclusive attribute of the universal.

The third coördinate in the Jewish nature is the need of physical comfort. Life is real and important to the Jew. His asceticism is always a sensual surrogate forced on him by his surroundings. It is never voluntary, never perverse, never dominant like the self-denial of the Anglo-Saxon. The Preacher has put down the immortal balance of the Jew. "In the day of prosperity be joyful, but in the day of adversity consider." The place of *comfort* in the philosophy of Spinoza is clear even to the title of his great book. It was no trivial matter to call a metaphysics "Ethics." The fact points to the Jewish need of practical application. Even the consciousness of God must serve a sensory end. As Spinoza says in another work *: he strives for knowledge "which shall enable him to enjoy continuous and supreme and unending happiness."

The Jew is the indefeasible realist. All his genius for seeing God must in the last analysis apply to the means of mortal life. The heights of his inspired speculation have ever been determined by the heights of the mundane barriers he needed to transcend in order to survive. So now, with the age of critical philosophy, of scientific method, of increased social toleration, his conditions changed. Gradually, the Christian earth became more real and urgent, the heavens grew dimmer. Gradually, men strove to apply their idea of heaven to the mundane present. The social

* De Intellectus Emendatione.

Revolution stirred on its long and bloody course. And a Jew, Karl Marx, appeared to give it form, substance, the passion of organic hope.

.   .   .   .

The three elements of which I have spoken reside generically in the Jewish mind. In the Jewish genius they rise coördinately to fruition. The paradox is solved. The masters of the Old Testament, Moses Maimonides, who was philosopher, priest, physician, Baruch Spinoza—were such Jews of genius. And through their like, the Jewish spirit lives. But in the majority of Jews, two of these elements go down before the sovereignty of one.

After all, a majority of Jews doubtless deemed Moses a scatter-brain and preferred Egypt: declined Cyrus' invitation to shake off the prestige and comforts of the Babylonian captivity. A majority of Jews, like a majority of other men and women, respond rather passively and simply to the external impulse of the world they live in. Certainly, a majority of Jews have done just that in the United States.

They came to America—mostly after 1880—with their sharpened wits and will-to-power, and America welcomed them and put these qualities to work. They came to America also with their love of God, but for such seed America was less fertile.

The Jew simply was caught up in the continental rhythm. He became a pioneer: in many ways, as we have seen, he was a Puritan already. He joined hands in the keen task of developing America. The power of wealth, the sanctity of money, were no secret to him. The sweets in the denial of sensuous indulgence when such indulgence was impossible or meant defeat, were no secret to him. The channeling of his mind upon the problems of practical dominion was an old channel to the Jew. Enormous incentives, these, in the American lands. He also poured outward: he also became spiritually poor: he also stripped for action. When the mystical Jew dies, the Jew is dead. The mystical Jew survived. But he slept. While the acquisitive Jew, the power-lusting Jew, the comfort-seeking Jew, at last unbarred from centuries of oppression and restraint, flooded upon a world that thirsted for his gifts.

The three directions of desire whose complex I have called Jewish are, of course, not uniquely so. The Jewish quality is rather their degree. The Jew is intense, high-keyed, above other men whose history has been a less continuous climax. And in his coming to America, he met an intensive need in an intensive land. His own intensity made him equal to the situation. The Jew, moreover, is tremendously adaptable in a superficial way. He can meet conditions: but at the end, he must stamp on them the marks of his own nature. Here again, the American adventure was auspicious. A vast, crude, virgin continent to bend to: his own passion for power and cultivation to impress upon it. Even the period of his coming was well-timed. His mystical obsession was out of place in pioneering. And he had come to America in an hour of revulsion against revealed theologies. Darwin had dealt the old God a blow. The geometric pace of mechanical power, of physical knowledge, for a time made men think that science was knowledge indeed, and that the shadows were retreating. The Jew in whom the genius for rational and empirical endeavor was always strong was dazzled along with the rest. He responded the more easily to pioneer demands, in an hour when his old mystical equipment seemed particularly futile. In this mystical equipment resided the culture of the Jew. As he dropped the first, the other fell away. Unlike the Latin and the Slav, he had in consequence no painful cultural assimilation to submit to. Like the Puritan's, his old cultural habits were already weak at his coming: his power to face new worlds to that extent enhanced. Thus, like the New Englander again, he played a rôle in the building of America out of all proportion to his numerical strength, because like him he was strategically placed.

The psychological history of the Jew in the United States is the process of his rather frenzied conformation to the land of his new opportunity: the sharpening of his means to power, the perfecting of his taste for comfort, the suppression of the mystical in his heart. For the mystical is never dead. It required the best activities of the Jewish mind to keep it under.

One of the early means was to find a substitute for the synagogue and for religion. The first generation still kept the Sabbath. The third is altogether "free." The middle generation went half way—with substitutes. As an example of this degenerate Judaism, none could serve us better than the "Societies for Ethical Culture," of which the first was founded in 1876 by Dr. Felix Adler. Adler's father was a Rabbi and the son was called to the same service. He went back to Germany—where he was born—to complete his studies. Modern empiricism brought the doubt. The doubt wiped most of the old slate clean. The young Doctor Adler came home to America empty. To what extent, let his own words tell: "Accordingly, on returning from abroad, my first action consisted in founding among men of my own or nearly my own age a little society which we ambitiously called a Union for the Higher Life, based on three tacit assumptions: sex purity, the principle of devoting the surplus of one's income beyond that required by one's own genuine needs to the elevation of the working class, and thirdly, continued intellectual development." Now, there is nothing remarkable about this sterile statement. What is significant is that a generation of American Jews looked upon this man as their spiritual father! Adler proceeded to evolve an adulterate religion. He avoided the concepts of God and Godhood: he declared Faith to be of no importance: he poised the world on an abstract notion of "personal worth" devoid of personality and worthless. Adler had met Socialism in Berlin. The "Moral Order" he came back with was a first worried effort on the part of the still healthy Jewish bourgeoisie to save the pickings for themselves. To it, he sacrificed Jehovah.

The main adherence of these Societies in New York and other American cities was among the prosperous

Jews who had shown themselves most apt to run the American race. Religious memories haunted these people. Most of them had been brought up in the Jewish church. They turned to Adler to give them a semblance of creed: one which would still the stirring of the Past, bring them no preoccupation to conflict with their affairs and, on the contrary, fit them the more aptly and the more politely for the life of respectable material dominion which America afforded. A completely commercialized religion: a religion, in other words, which was no religion at all, since all the mystery of life, all the harmony of sense, all the immanence of God were deleted from it: and in their place a quiet, moral code destined to make good citizens of eager pioneers. In Spinoza, *Ethics* had meant the lifting up of consciousness to the universal, since for so great a soul no lesser contemplation could serve human joy. With these others, *Ethics* meant the complete excision of all that was mystical, all that in any way could debauch the human interest from the immediate affairs of a commercial world. These Jews were afraid of religion, even to the extent of not daring openly to do without it. "The Society for Ethical Culture" met their problem. It was free not only of the suppressed demands of the Jewish soul, but even of the odium of the Jewish name.*

---

* It is perhaps only fair to repeat that a similar adulteration had long since gone on in many Protestant churches. One that engages me most is the gospel of the "Finite God," now preached by certain forward-looking ministers, and glorified by no less a man than H. G. Wells. The idea behind the Finite God is to effect a compromise between our Reason which tells us that this is an

Meantime, the Jew was spreading out. He filled our schools, he filled our public colleges, he filled the laboratories of science. He knew, like any pioneer, that the mystery and the experience of life were poison. He knew that the best defense from the subtle promptings of his race lay in the passionate devotion to rational pursuits. He poured into the medical colleges and law schools. He joined hands with the Irish in Tammany Hall and became a practical politician. He discovered Pragmatism and reduced it to its most acrid and cynical dogmas of utilitarian supineness. And everything he did, he did a little more intensely, a little more like the fanatic, than his brothers. For not alone was his nature intrinsically pitched at a high key: he needed the added stress in order to combat the mystical yearnings which his reason covered.

Here, then, this strange phenomenon of our present day! the anæsthetic Jew. The literal-minded Gentile is as a rule content with his world of facts: secure in it. The literal-minded Jew is a Jew unbalanced. He declared defensive war against the other side: particu-

imperfect world and our lurking desire for some sort of worship. An Infinite God could not be held responsible for such a mess as *Science* (so they say) tells us this suffering world is. Let a finite God take his place—the credit and the blame. By positing a deity who is almost as weak and fumbling as ourselves, like ourselves "on-the-make"—(a dash here of pseudo-Bergsonianism), we avoid the issue. Of course, such a God is a sop thrown by King Reason to abject intuition. He is a product of a prevailing intellectual arrogance, by no means to be found among superior men of science, which will admit nothing beyond the range of rational adventure. To say that such a God is an absurdity, a distinctly *a-religious* invention, seems to me not to say too much.

larly against religion and art. We have seen a similar psychic process in Mark Twain. Himself an intuitive and "tender-minded" man, he held to his forced rank in the frontiering world by denial of his nature— and by violent attack when it appeared in others. So the Jew, electing to worship power, achieve comfort, suppressed the God in him, and by way of it, denied the God in others. Instinctively, he went out in arms against all approach, spiritual, æsthetic, which might stir in himself the senses he denied. A simple process of transference of which the subject only remains unaware.

Jews of this sort have played a great part in the recent intellectual life of the United States. They are bitter, ironic, passionately logical. And the camps of the Enemy fascinate them so, they cannot keep away. They become critics of the arts. They consort with artists: study the anatomy of æsthetics: and from the strategy of close acquaintance subtly inspire the distrust of art, prove art is dying, teach how trivial an affair art has become.

Some of these men are mere disappointed artists: souls bitter at their own self-treachery. Others are deeply sincere and brilliantly equipped.* They have observed the spiritual disarray of the last thirty years: they have become submerged in it, above their eyes. They cannot see beyond the palpable failure of the present. And they are strengthened in their doctrine

* Among them—perhaps the most imposing and influential, by reason of his high integrity, intellectual power and close association with the art movements, here and abroad, of recent years— is Leo Stein.

of despair by the artists whom they know. For those
artists are, in large part, weak and loveless. They,
too, have innerly given up the fight against the pioneering rhythm: emotionally accepted the prevailing Puritan contempt. But in them, the critical faculties have
not harmonized desire and conviction. Their hearts
beat to the Puritan command. Their minds disobey.
They produce art lacking in love and vision. And
the more critical, the stronger-minded Jew seeing their
pathetic failures, is encouraged in his at least rational
despair.

Not alone the examples of modern life, as well the
modern tools of thought are on hand to help—and
to create the anæsthetic Jew, the Jew who has turned
all the passion of his blood against the vision which
has preserved him. He grasps at the discoveries of
science—whose philosophical inconsequence the true
scientist is foremost in avowing—in order to sneer
at the mysteries beyond. He quotes the new analytical psychology in order to prove the spiritual apper-
ceptions of mankind mere symptoms of neurosis.

In their bitter arrogance, the truth about these
men is clear enough. They are defending their conscious position against the encroachment of unconscious doubts. For these pragmatic doctrines—these
assumptions of the falsity of faith and the futility of
art—pander to their need of comfort: *the comfort
of the Limit*. Science has put up a nice, small room,
and lighted it quite well. Outside, as ever, rolls the
illimitable world—the world which Jews have ever
needed to explore. But these men have been made

weary by their freedom, have become spiritually weak in the new flowing-forth of their desires. The wider universe haunts them and sings to their blood. So they deny it: prove desperately that it does not exist and that the limits of the fitful glow of their experimental candle are the limits of all life. Equally, these doctrines pander to their need of power. A giant, as there have been giants among the Jews, lets his vision out upon infinity and embraces that. These depleted minds are still ambitious, they still yearn to possess what they perceive. Since they are weak, therefore, they solve the problem by perceiving less. They exercise power in the little spaces of the reasonable world. It is sweet for them to hold there are no spaces beyond.

So the passive response of the Jew to the traditional American demand is complicated by the vast spiritual sacrifice which the Jew peculiarly must make. The Jewish paradox—the Jewish nature—is broken up. This sacrifice means conflict. This conflict adds to the intensity of Jewish adaptation. For if the Jew went less wilfully on his elected way, the suppressed need of his life would rise and swing him elsewhere, and he might not go that way at all.

.   .   .   .

This rich element, then, flung into the many others to make the American chaos. Sons of an ancient Sacrifice—these aggressive and worldly and compromising men who fill our markets and our professions. But let it not be overlooked: the Jew who dwindles himself down to these is sick and restless. The stifled

Will is ready to burst forth. And in the most degraded families of Jews, you find them: solitary sons and daughters, stirring and rebellious—outposts—in whom that Will has become once more incarnate.

During eight decades of the Nineteenth Century, the human spirit struggled against the incoming tide of mechanical and industrial aberration. Nietzsche, Flaubert, Whitman, Tolstoi, Dostoievski—such were the last giants to float. Then the world went under. The Machine, the sweep of material aggrandizement which the Machine made possible—offered a delirious game upon which the Occidental world poured its passions. We are beginning to understand what that vast flood has swept away. The old community of art, the old worship of God, the old economic orders. But more: the flood has swept away the frenzied material obsession which first loosed the flood. Quite as dead as the old idolatries is the heresy of the dominion of empirical thought: quite as futile as the art of the old secluded classes, has become the arrogant belief that art and religion can be dispensed with. . . .

In the American chaos the Jew went under. We shall see how, in the American birth, he rises up.

IV. THE LAND OF BURIED CULTURES

IF I relate this trivial scene, the reason is that all America reminds me of it. At Pueblo, Colorado, I took a motor-bus. Pueblo belongs to that vast tract, summing a million of square miles, which the United States conquered from Mexico in 1848. In the bus with me are Mexicans and one Anglo-Saxon. The Mexicans talk much, gesticulate. The men among them wear bright colors. The women are dressed in black, but their eyes are deep and slow like shaded summer pools in which many colors have fallen, and their black hair is blue. The Anglo-Saxon is quiet and sallow and wealthier than all the rest of us together. The bus swings out from the dirty industrial town. It scoots over the roll of a hill, and there before us is the thing I mean. . . . Beyond, against the sun rise the vast chimneys of the steel-mills. They stand on the brow of a hill. A dozen shafts belch smoke into the skies. The sun lies on the battlemented buildings and makes them bright and makes them tower. Beneath, the hill falls away in arid ground: a sterile earthen waste whose strength seems to have been sucked to the triumphing mills above. And in this scoop of desolation, scattered adobe huts: colored like the waste earth, and stained with soot, and lost in both of them. The huts are in shadow. The sun and the hill's summit draw all the color of the skies upon the steel-mills.

These are the homes of Mexicans to whom once this land belonged. They were unable to crown their earth with factories. Now, they shovel coal, and the smoke of their shoveling is black upon their valleys.

Steel-mills are not everywhere in the old Mexican lands of the United States. But the product of the steel-mills, and the spirit of the steel. When the soot is absent, the 'dobe houses are not soiled. They gleam like gold under the hot blue skies. They are of the earth on which they lie: of the earth of these people and of their hands: harmonious, therefore, beautiful. And one can go into them, marvelous fresh in summer, marvelous warm in winter, and glimpse a buried world.

The Mexican was not an ideal pioneer. He became attached to his soil and loved it, and drew pleasure and drew beauty from it. This proves that he was not an ideal pioneer, who must be forever ready to move on, must have more "serious" ambitions. The towns of the Mexican in the American South-West are sparse. Scattered about are newer centers—the dwellings of the "gringoes." Everywhere you will find them: houses of flat timber, scantily daubed in store-paint, or not painted at all and already eaten by the weather. Usually these houses have flat roofs. A single sheet of tin makes them look gabled from the front. They suggest impermanence, indifference to nature, absorption in other matters. But the Mexican's 'dobe gives us his inner life. Here a man has settled down and sought happiness in harmony with his surroundings: sought life by cultivation, rather than exploitation.

There is a terrible humility in these squat, straw-grained homes with their bright blue shutters and their crimson flowers. And if you meet the Mexican who lives in them, you realize that there is tragedy. For the Mexican is cowed, and is beaten. He moves about like one who feels himself a dog among men. He bends the neck to the steel-mill and to the hard, keen masters who are the makers of steel. The Americans live in ugly houses, so he comes to despise the intimate temper that made him beautify his own. The Americans go to the Machine for their pleasure as well as for their food. So he comes to despise the labor of his hand. Nothing that is his meets the approval of the "gringoes." He is a "greaser," a half-breed, a "nigger." The Americans are stronger and the Americans do not respect him. What then will it gain him to respect himself? The Mexican, in the United States, sinks thus into the certain ways of one who has lost his faith and given up his pride. He becomes dissolute, shiftless, insolent and cringing. He falls victim to his suppressed hot passions. He joins mystic orders like the "Penitentes"—decadent relics of the Flagellants of Spain—whose bloody sacrificial rites give perverse satisfaction to his misery and fear.

And yet, those portions of the South-West which the Mexican had already settled when the American broke in with his superior artillery, still bear his stamp. For he alone had won a certain culture from the arid soil of that high country. And it is the

American who culturally submits. The Mexican met the Indian and learned from him. Much of what is beautiful in Mexican life has its clear source in the ancient Indian cultures. But sincere adaptation is creation. The Mexican has made the 'dobe town his own. He has added his color and his mood to it. With Mexican pottery, Mexican weaving, Mexican jewelry, it is the same. The true marriage of the Indian and the Spaniard has brought about a native culture. The lowly Mexican is articulate, the lordly American is not. For the Mexican has really dwelt with his soil, cultivated his spirit in it, not alone his maize. He has stooped to conquer. And when you enter the homes of the occasional intelligent Americans of the South-West, you realize how truly the whipped race has won. The walls that cool or warm you, the rug you step on, the food you eat proclaim the Mexican master.

The pity is that his mastery should be so brief and superficial. The American did not absorb or learn. In his hands, the integral expressions of Mexican life—their remarkable harmony with the native American world—become toys of the picturesque, motives for cheap commercial imitation. And conversely, the growing dominion of the "gringo" is stamping out the impulse from which this native culture sprang. Soon, it will have fled southward over the American Border. There are plenty of collectors to rage like locusts through the New Mexican and South-Californian hills, and make their blight of *Santas* and pottery and blankets. But America was too long insulated from this spiritual wealth that flowered along the edges of the Great Desert. It had no eyes for the loveliness of 'dobe towns, nor for the fire of this people that still burns under the ban of the Industrial world like jewels in the dark. And now that America is readier to see and learn, the Mexican is already lost in the spell of the tin-can and the lithograph. For what has been buried must die surely.

.   .   .   .

Some day some one who is fitted for the task will take the subject of this Chapter and make a book of it. He will study the cultures of the German, the Latin, the Celt, the Slav, the Anglo-Saxon and the African on the American continent: plot their reactions one upon the other, and their disappearance as integral worlds in the vast puddling of our pioneering life. I have no space and no knowledge for so huge a picture. I must be content with the suggestion of a single curve.

The March of the white man across the continent has been the flowing of a Stream. As the Stream flowed, it overwhelmed the life that stood in its way. All life opposing was swept within its general current. But also, the varied life that had made up the Stream, had given to it its force, soon lost its variance and was merged.

Puritanism in its historic form had controlled the direction of pioneering. Now the continental impulse drew in new life from Europe. New England was Puritan no longer. But even the scattered vanguards of New England which had established Puritan thought throughout the land came to be crushed beneath the very might which in an earlier form had sent them forth. The culture of Puritanism, for all its rigidity and dogma, had been a living thing. It met the resources of America and American Industrialism was the issue. The Puritan ways of life and thought and measure were taken over. They fitted the new, more vigorous, more realistic pioneering form. American Industrialism is the new Puritanism, the true Puritanism of our day. As we use the word throughout the ensuing chapters, let us forever bear in mind the Puritan content that goes along. Meantime, the old Puritan form which still survived from the hegemony of Boston came to be submerged. The old Puritanism, the Puritanism of New England, scattered throughout America, was a buried culture. . . .

If, in whatever part of the United States you are, you wish to make the personal acquaintance of this buried culture, go to a meeting of the Reverend Billy Sunday. Sunday himself for all his gesticulations savors of the grave. He is a wiry, nervous fellow, with the nose of a fox-terrier and the voice of a damaged phonograph. He was once a professional baseball player. Now he is America's most renowned Evangelist. The town to which he comes with his stridulous message builds him a Tabernacle that seats ten thousand. And Mr. Sunday fills it two times daily. The Protestant churches of the city—with certain illustrious exceptions—cower to his doorstep and beg him to refill their pews. He does so. His methods are a long cry from the evangelism of John Wesley. But in this they are in the direct succession: the old exhorters gave to the people what they wanted, and so does Mr. Sunday. He gives them vaudeville, acrobatics, profanity and the suggestion of lascivious subjects. Disguised of course beneath the semblance of a sermon. The Puritan dare not take sugar. So Mr. Sunday coats his drams of sweetness with the gall of precept. Then the Puritan can swallow what his age-long "naysaying" stomach is too weak to accept "straight." He is forbidden to dance: so Mr. Sunday, in describing the hellishness of saltatory movements, dances for him. He is forbidden to drink and swear: so Mr. Sunday flies into a drunken frenzy of damning words to paint him the Hell that drink and swearing lead to. He must not covet woman: so Mr. Sunday gives suggestive discourse upon low-neck gowns, the proximity of bodies in the dance, the theme of "vampire" dramas, and the possibilities of unlighted theaters with close seats.

But I do not mean to dwell here on the deep meaning of many of this preacher's antics: nor on the not-too-hidden lure in them that draws the multitudes to listen to his words.* The point is this: I have

---

* Let me quote from an old article of mine, published in *The Seven Arts* of July, 1917, at the time of Mr. Sunday's visit to New York:

"The success of Billy Sunday is due to the use of what, in pathology, is known as the *conversion-mechanism:*—the channeling of an instinctive desire away from an expression that is forbidden to one that is disguised and not forbidden. It is unsafe to give open leash to sexuality, so turn the passion into the fear of Hell and glut your worry by 'hitting the trail.' It is uneconomic to get

heard Mr. Sunday speak in cities separated by a thousand miles, and I have noticed that his audience is always one! In the most varied cities of the North, the nature of his public never changes. For Mr. Sunday is a magnet that draws New England.

Now, when you study these long, rigid rows of desiccated men and women, you feel that you are in the presence of some form of life that has hardened but not grown, and over which the world has passed. The sawdust Tabernacle is possibly in Chicago. Step outside, chat with the policeman, joke with a newsboy, and Chicago comes to you once more: its tang, its vibrance. But within, this multitude of creatures seems to have come from some other world that has not heard of metropolitan Chicago. Look at them well. Their jaws are rigid. Their eyes are as lead, they have so long denied the beauties of the world. Their complexions are like greasy ash. On the brow of the young man is the bland complacency of a feeble mind, and the shoulders of the girl twitch with the energy she dares not utter. These people are descendants of Puritan New England. They have denied life so splendidly that even they have denied Industrialism. Now they live in Illinois or Indiana. But they are still keyed to the petty possessiveness of the Colonial New

drunk on alcohol, so wave a flag and get drunk on God. It may be natural to lose your temper with your brother, but it is less dangerous to get mad at the Devil. Such his method. And one need only remark the constantly recurring wreath of smile on the terrier-like countenance of Mr. Sunday to realize what good fun it must be to have his sort of 'religion' in a materialistic and fun-denying world. The neurotic satisfies himself with a set of distorted symptoms in place of an unfriendly and hard reality. . . ."

100

England town. Their veins have hardened. Their blood has soured. The great Roger Williams and Jonathan Edwards have become this Reverend Billy. But though Industrialism circles them, you have but to look at them to realize the power of inertia that they wield. They are not manifest upon the streets, these cavernous men and women. But the acid of their souls eats through America. No politician can hope for office against their pleasure. No book can be sold that shocks them. They have but recently decided, by Constitutional Amendment, that no beer shall defile American lips. In ways devious and clear, they command from the Tomb.

Thus has the pioneering Stream buried the Puritan —buried the great culture which he produced nearly three centuries ago. Behold it now, burying even the pioneer!

People from the vital Middle-west, as well as vital people from the Pacific slope who have escaped eastward, often ask the question: "What is wrong with the Southern half of California?" The citizen of Los Angeles will answer that, far from wrong, everything there is perfect. Fifty years ago, he will tell you, Southern California was a desert. Cactus and yucca grew where now the orange blooms. Los Angeles was a low Mexican 'dobe village and is now the biggest city west of St. Louis. Southern California is rich. Even the Mexican prospers, now that the Yankee has made the water flow through his old desert. Its oranges and prunes are the biggest, its flowers are the brightest. Its climate is the most equable.

And it lays claim to being one of the chief art-centers of the country. . . . So speaks the Angelano. And he speaks true. He has indeed turned his land into a garden. And even if his boasting about the weather may seem a trifle irreligious to the New Yorker, his claim to art ascendency may hold. For Los Angeles is the home of the motion-picture: is the home of our dearest dramatic artist, Charlie Chaplin.*

And yet—and yet—something is grievously amiss in Elysian Southern California. Every one who goes there feels it. It should not be hard to place. But it is a thing so tenuous, that it eludes description. It is a matter of temperament, it is a fault—a want—of personality. Southern California, for all its fruits and flowers, lacks color and perfume. Its people, despite their sleek accomplishments, are without force, almost without desire.

Since the Angelano boasts so much, let us observe his city. About the Plaza live the buried Mexicans. An old dirty part of town: crumbling 'dobe houses, redolent wine-shops, donkeys and sombrero'd greasers clustered under the palms and nut-trees of a sleepy Square. Yes: the Angelano may be right. Life glows here, somehow, beneath this ruddy dirt. But he protests. This is not the splendor of which he speaks. "Mexican town" is being swept away by the broom of progress. Soon, thank Heaven, it will be forgotten. Here is our modern city.

Endless avenues strewn with prim bungalows.

* Charlie Chaplin was born near London, in 1888. Yet America may claim him perhaps properly for her own. See Chapter VIII

Asphalt gleaming: tropic palms jutting up from occidental pavements. Carlines clanging through low distances of empty streets, patches of squatter-village not yet overtaken by the march of the bungalow, a filthy lane nodding in castor-bushes, then once more the flat tidiness of little houses, little flower-plots and little palms. The city's center is a clean and forceless imitation, as in most Western cities, of the Chicago "Loop."* Overhead, the passion of sapphire sky. Underneath, swarms of bleached men and women, in bleached clothes, hurrying to dinner.

All cities speak. Some roar, some shrill, some whisper. Los Angeles has no voice. Its vast expanse of pretty houses and wide gutters and inept palms suggests the smile of an empty face. Los Angeles is not a city. It is a country town that has outgrown its rural voice and found no other. One has the sense, walking its myriad, well-paved miles, that there lacks the vibrance of real thought, the stir of passion. Los Angeles somehow has no direction. One feels that its crowded central streets are not a head, but a stomach. One understands that its inhabitants are rows of naughts made valid by no integer of purpose.

What is the reason? Its streets are full of bustle, its papers are full of headlines. Why is it in so mysterious a way *devoid* of life? In groping for an answer, I thought of the huge California orange. For many years, the growers had bent their energy toward

* The center of Chicago is so known because all the elevated railroad lines of the immense city converge upon it and encircle a restricted area within which banks, offices, hotels, theaters, restaurants cluster as in an old walled town.

bigness. Here was the product. Huge, indeed, but without flavor. The virtue of the fruit—its capacity of sun—had gone to size. If one dared use the term, the vast and juiceless California fruit was an *extra-verted thing!* * * * And then, I thought of the mountainous energy which the Californian had been driven to expend before he reached his desert on the Pacific coast, and before that desert turned under his hand into a garden. And it seemed that I understood.

Here was the remotest reach of pioneering, where it fell westward from the Sierras. It had to stop. There was no farther way. The Orient was not a gate but a bar. In the North, newer incentives were already there to transform the balked energy of the frontiersman. The industrial incentives: mining and lumbering and the bridling of great rivers. Not so in the South. Industrialism was still beyond. The pioneer was left to his own resources. And he had none. His energy could not transform, so it drooped. For it is and ever was resourceless, save in the following of a horizon. The air of Southern California is dry. The Pacific surface is not as saline as the Atlantic Ocean. No Gulf Stream murks the sky. A preservative air is that of Southern California. And in it, like the corpse of some vast animal, the pioneer lies supine but in good condition: isolated from all hostile agents, a pretty specimen for the social student. His one activity, the hewing of roads beyond the hills, is gone. Behold his spirit in repose. . . .

It is sterile. Its agitation begets chill sparks of brilliance, but no good human heat. It is complacent.

It has the assurance that uncovered continents here turned to the sole use of hiding all subjective knowledge. It cannot work, but also it cannot play, and also it cannot sleep. The siesta of Spain is as foreign to it as the carnival of Nice or the frenzy of Chicago. It can no longer blaze a trail: but it is ignorant of dreams. Next door to it is the Orient. Somehow, the deep mysteries of India have trickled in: they become shallow cults designed to flick away the idle energies of its women. It has no receptivity. It turns its back on China and Japan, or faces them to make long noses. But it is also insulated from main America. The books of Europe inspire it to facile imitation. It looks at the East furtively over one shoulder. It faces nowhere: least of all, it faces itself.*

So here in California, the student may behold this rare laboratory specimen: the very body of the pioneer, buried in its inertia, isolate, preserved. A helpless thing with a noble past. But if I speak so harshly of what is but a fact, I am less reluctant since already that fact is disappearing. The War has brought to California the industrialism which long before had spilled its smoke over Washington and Oregon. San Diego is a great shipyard. New railways pour in metal

* San Francisco presents a cheerier aspect:—a maze of mostly wooden and quite ugly houses tumbling about hills so delightful that the city is delightful also. The topography of San Francisco is indefeasibly lovely. And the town, too, is full of life, full of climaxes of color. Why? Alas for the answer. Because of the Chinese and Japanese, Mexicans and Spaniards and Italians. The charm of San Francisco is almost wholly due to the non-Anglo-Saxon elements which contribute restaurants, theaters, old Squares, inimitable shops—or to the hills and the Bay and the Golden Gate upon the Sea.

and men. I am no apologist for the industrial chaos. But we shall see how a world is being born of it. And surely there is no like hope in the Nirvana of the buried pioneer. California starts on the bitter cycle of American preculture. It will writhe in filth and smoke: groan with disorder. And then, some day, as with the rest of us, its complacency will break, and it will begin to live.

．　　．　　．　　．　　．　　．　　．

The European cultures, swept to America and there buried, were half-killed by the mere uprooting. They were never American: they could never live *in* America. The principle of death carried them from Europe: gave them the mere *coup de grâce* when they made their fitful stand for survival in a pioneering world. The Puritan culture also was an impermanent life. It grew to meet a particular condition: a condition at best fleeting and superficial.

But a great and varied cultural world already lay upon America before the coming of the pioneer. America was peopled. From the Northwestern tip (in all probability), prehistoric tribes had beaten their way down from Asia. In each of ten thousand stations, from Alaska to the Horn, some of them had settled and made a world: others had spread away until two continents were alive. In places, these dim voyagers seem either to have lost their ancient cultures, or at least to have achieved no great new one. In other places, they gradually fixed in a cultural state perhaps not far —materially and spiritually—from the state of the early pastoral Hebrews. But there were regions in

106

which there lifted up from the vast ethnic bed great peoples: fashioners of beauty, masters of communal order, worshipers of a true God.

Everywhere, the cultures which we call Indian—symbolizing and perpetuating in the false name our ignorance—were of a spiritual nature: tended in a degree we can measure toward spiritual greatness. And everywhere, these cultures were buried by the Caucasian floods.

In the Latin lands, not buried altogether. These pioneers were not pioneers enough, not dense enough in their pouring masses, to blot the Indian away. Two worlds swirled in conflict and compounded. An amalgam of strife and unending flux explains the feverish state of South America and Mexico, where the white masters are not strong enough to destroy: the half-destroyed not strong enough to rise up and master.

But in America—our land—the work is well done. Where we may walk, in Maine, in Florida, in Oregon, in Texas, we walk a land that is a place of death. Beneath our feet, lie buried the remains of a human world. . . .

In the central lands of Yucatan and Guatamala, this world perhaps reached its apogee. The Mayas builded great cities, and made beauty out of rock and upon walls, for whose like in profundity of form one must go back to India and Egypt. They wrote books that are still undeciphered, since the zeal of the Jesuits succeeded in destroying their vast bulk. But the ruins of their greatness in the tropic forests are not hard to read. They bespeak a rich and fertile people, accomplished in spiritual and æsthetic works. After their might had set, came the Aztecs and their neighbors. They builded a great nation in Mexico. And upon the zenith of this, Hernan Cortes swooped down with his Spanish muskets and blotted them out. The Spaniards came from a feudal world: a world of tyranny and dynastic greed. They could see in the splendor of the Mexican pueblos no system other than their own. They bore back to Europe glowing tales of the Empire of the Aztecs, of the Emperor Montezuma. They were radically wrong. But indolence and ill-will have made their lies perpetual. The American historian Prescott, in his book, *The Conquest of Mexico*, has stabilized the whole tissue of ignorant confections which were perhaps excusable in the pioneering and preoccupied Spaniards. The child accepts these falsehoods, even now, in the American schools.

The Aztecs had no Empire. Montezuma was no Emperor. Empire and Kingdom were unknown to the Indian world. The Aztecs formed a confederacy of free nations, much like that of the Iroquois. Their states were founded upon fairly democratic suffrage: their lands were communal. Montezuma was their *teuctli*—war-chief, or their *tlatoani*—speaker of the Council. He was chosen by the Gentes of the Three Great Nations. Save on the field of battle, he was forever under the control of the Chiefs of Council. At all times he was subject to removal, and at no time did his powers encroach upon the civil rights of the community.

The entire sense of this ancient Indian life was contrary to our feudal-economic point of view. The lands were plotted off, and each man who was a toiler was as well an owner. The cities were divided into familial estates, and each woman who was a mother had her share. The *cacique*—spiritual chief—was the true head of his people.

Such was the Confederation of the Aztecs which the Spaniards reduced to an anarchy of vindictive, miserable tribes. Such, in essence, was the way of all the Indian nations, South and North, whom the pioneer progressively beat down into their present weakness.

The Indian is a savage only by the materialistic measure of the Caucasian. His one inferiority lay in his lack of metal weapons. Like the white man, the stages of his culture varied. In the warmer climates, he created beautiful and lasting civilizations. In the plains of the North he was more the wanderer. Here his life had the fluidity of fertile streams. But everywhere, he had one fatal weakness: he knew not iron. And everywhere, his cultural possessions, his way of meeting life agreed. Whether he dwelt in populous cities or in *tepees*, he lived in a spiritual world so true and so profound, that the heel of the pioneer has even now not wholly stamped it out.

The American prefers not to dwell on the effect of the white invasion upon the Indian nature. The white man called the Indian bloody, treacherous. And yet he merely tried to defend his world. And as he found his arrows shattered by the iron monsters of the pioneer, he did indeed grow desperate, at times cruel. But fortunately, the Indian is not yet gone. And in his spirit, his works, his physiognomy to-day—after centuries of violence, centuries of brutal contact with cultures he was helpless to forefend—we may read the answer to our ignorance.

Many of the Indian nations have succumbed. The fluent ways of the plains people were least equipped to resist the Caucasian floods. Great tribes have disappeared, either by intermarriage or by the wastage of a hostile life. The American authorities wage relentless war upon the Indian customs. By law and schooling, they conclude to-day the work of yesterday's invasion. And many are their victims. But although the entire question of saving a world so wistful, so alien as the Indian, in our materialistic age, seems vain, yet it is not too late to glimpse what that world was.

In the Southwest this purpose is perhaps best answered.

The Rocky Mountains cast their Southern spurs through a great dry land. Here, solitary rivers like the Rio Grande combat the desert. And along the valleys of these streams, the Pueblo peoples, like them who came before, now live in cities. These cities reach back to prehistoric times. In canyons like *Pajarito* and that of the *Rito de los Frijoles* such scholars as Dr. E. L. Hewett* have unearthed the remains of vast communities, that were already dead when the Spaniards landed. Doubtless the progressive desiccation of all these valleys drove life away. But they have left their story. The canyons run roughly east and west, pouring their steep streams into the Rio Grande. Upon

* See Note at end of Chapter.

the northern talus, the first men cut rooms in the soft rock. And then, as their cunning grew, they built houses of several stories against the cliffs. They hollowed out great *kivas*—the silent places where they sought the Truth in meditation—they timbered and plastered their rooms: and at last in the verdant valleys erected great community houses, sometimes of more than twelve hundred chambers.

One can still clamber up the steep sides of these canyons, and dwell in the dwellings of these people: see the smoke of their passed fires and the pictures that they carved, and the gorgeous pottery that they made. And one can look southward across the gap, over their tree-tops, and see their outer world. Or descend, as they did, by ladder into the sacred *kivas* and seek out their spirits.

And then one can go down to the main valley of the Rio Grande, and know the cities of the Indians to-day.

Here, in this country below the desert, live three layers of men. The American who conquered the Mexican, on top: the Mexican who conquered the Indian, upon the middle ground: beneath, the Indian himself.

The Pueblo Indian has preserved his culture admirably. He does not intermarry. He has never been warlike, though he has fought. And he has met the Catholic invasion by a clever compromise. Technically, he is Catholic. He begins his public ceremonials with an obeisance before the Christian altar, listens carefully to the Priest who has come down from the nearest Mexican village to preach the horrors of infidelity

—and then, falling back upon his own religion, he forgets the rest.

He lives in battlemented houses, mounting in towns like Taos five stories high. He has his buried *kivas* where the youth and the old men must spend a certain portion of their days in prayer and where the spiritual father, the *cacique*, quite as in the days of the Pajaritans and the Aztecs, prepares the lustral functions. Strange, tragical places are these old Pueblos with their high blank walls against the Stranger. The upper walls are reached by ladders that stand against the adobe flanks and rise from the many roofs to the roofs above. Here, at the sun's setting, the men sit on the highest summit of their building, wrapped in white sheets, and greet the night. And then, they enter down, also by ladders, into the apartments that belong to their mothers and their wives.

There are always two great groups of buildings, and between them usually runs a stream whose water the Indian reveres as the living element which he channels across baked fields and by whose magic the fields grow green and give forth corn and wheat. In the one group of buildings, live the Summer-people, presided over by their *cacique:* in the other, live the Winter-people who with their *cacique* have charge of all the ceremonies and duties of the Winter. These priests are the masters, if masters there are. Wealth and public responsibility are evenly divided. To the women belongs the Town: they must keep it comfortable and clean. To the men belong the fields: they must make them give forth food, and defend them again invasion.

Presiding over this life and forever near is Nature. The *cacique* is the interpreter between Nature and his people. Indian religion does not vary greatly. It is not a religion of sacrifice or egoistic prayer, as the missionaries taught us. The Indian believes that he must live in harmony with Nature, and its Great Spirit. If he does, he will have good hunting, he will have good harvest, he will have good children. But the way to harmony with the Great Spirit is not through magic. It is a *subjective* matter. If he lives naturally, if his thoughts are worshipful and pure, then his fields will yield good crops. His magic is not, as in most religions, the tricky power of men over their gods. It lies in the power of Nature herself to yield corn from irrigation, to yield meat in game. The Indian therefore does not pray to his God for direct favors. He prays for harmony between himself and the mysterious forces that surround him: of which he is. For he has learned that from this harmony comes health.

To this end, he has his ceremonies: dances and songs for the several seasons to turn his mind into the paths of fellowship with the Great Spirit. These ceremonies form the greater portion of his art. The dances are profoundly organized æsthetic units. The music is subtle, naked, full of intricate and measured strength. The costuming is rich with symbolic fancy, and yet simple, lovely to the eye. The refinement of countless generations informs these arts: they are the expression of a people schooled in the harsh struggle of existence who have nonetheless won from their sobriety of life a margin of joy and of meditation.

The Indian art is classic, if any art is classic. Its dynamics are reserved for the inward meaning. Its surface has the polish of ancient custom. Its content is the pure emotional experience of a people who have for ages sublimated their desire above the possessive into the creative realm. The uncorrupted Indian knows no individual poverty or wealth. All of his tribe is either rich or poor. He has no politics. He has no dynastic or industrial intrigue—although of course personal and fraternal intrigue does exist. His physical world is fixed. And in consequence all his energies beyond the measure of his daily toil rise ineluctably to spiritual consciousness: flow to consideration of his place and part in Nature, into the business of beauty. In some Indian tongues, one word serves for *happiness* and *beauty*. How significant this is! How it determines the direction of the Indian's activity which, as we know, is the mere currency of his search for happiness. His search for beauty!

The touch of this is upon all his works. It is upon his dwellings, upon his pottery, upon his jewelry and ceremonials and dress. But most impressively of all, the touch of this preoccupation is upon his person. The bearing of the Indian is rythmical and reticent, like his dancing and his music. His body is erect and fluent, symbol of his greatest striving: to achieve an inner harmony with the living world. The proud, massive power of his features is no less than the outward mark of that harmony which his race has won. The Indian girl is gentle, timid, musical in the flutter of her hands and the note of her voice. Her eyes are too open

114

to meet the gaze of the stranger. They would pour all the limpidity of her soul upon him. She moves hidden in black shawls * from the sun's passion that would exhaust her own. But when she is a woman and a mother, her slender grace spreads into buxom ease. She is still rather silent, but her form welcomes fellowship and work. She depicts the homely realism of Indian life. The slow, sure march of her mate, his indrawn lips and searching eyes suggest the majesty of long silences in prayer.

The Indian is dying and is doomed. There can be no question of this. There need be no sentimentality. It may seem unjust that a spiritual culture so fine as his should be blotted out before the iron march of the Caucasian. It may seem the very irony of progress. But Justice is an anthropomorphic fancy. And Progress is the measure of children for their own rollicking. The white man came with his material prowess, and under the steel hail of his onslaught the world of the Indian, its profound residence in Nature, lies maimed and buried. No one knows this better, meets this more fearlessly than the Indian himself.

It seems to me that in his final gesture toward the white swarms that are wiping him away, the Indian has proved the temper of his breeding. He no longer dreams of physical resistance. Nature, which he so deeply understands, has never seemed to him a tender being. It brought him the snows of winter, the droughts of summer, the ravages of beast and flame. Now, this

---

* These shawls are originally Mexican. There has been true cultural exchange between the Indian and the Latin.

same Nature has brought the ravage of the white man
also. The Indian will be destroyed. But his love for
the laws of life, the pride of his own being before the
mysteries that dispose, remain with him. He withdraws forever farther within himself. He makes his
sanctuary of silent meditation deeper from the encroachment of the hostile human world. And holding
up his head, he meets the Storm.*

* It is unfortunately true that American indifference to this
buried culture shows no wide sign of abatement. Much sentiment is gushed over the traces of the "noble red man." The attitude of the average American school alternates between con-
temptuous and lyrical ignorance. Nowhere is there a widespread
effort to *study* the Indian culture as a native fact from which vast
spiritual wealth might still be mined. The Indian Office of the
United States is brutal and venal. It does not disguise its will to
stamp out the Indian's dances, cut his long hair and "civilize" him
out of existence. In centers of the great Pueblo district of New
Mexico, like Taos or Santa Fé, colonies of artists, seekers after
the "picturesque," have gathered. They paint Indians in costume,
they collect blankets to decorate their walls. As an æsthetic force
they are, in my judgment, beneath notice. They do not understand
or absorb. Like all painters of the "picturesque," they are mere
truants from reality.
There is, however, a great exception to this condemnatory
note. Dr. Edgar Lee Hewett (born on a farm in Warren County,
Illinois, 1865) is the director of the School of American Research
of the Archæological Society of America. He is a great
student of the indigenous cultures. But he is far more. He is
a remarkable friend of the living Indian. His spirit is strangely
akin to theirs. He lives near them, he speaks their tongue, he
knows their needs. He has done more than any other man of
whom I know to preserve the Indian's self-respect, hearten him to
new artistic and self-expressive effort, reinforce his true religious
life. More than any Caucasian he typifies the belated effort to
lift up the really horrible condition of the Indian in a hostile
world which was his own. And he achieves this, simply by a deep
understanding and a great respect. Dr. Hewett belongs, despite
his age, to the uprising generation whom we shall first examine in
the following Chapter. He should have been included among the
Chicago poets. For, essentially, he is a poet. . . .

V. CHICAGO

SURELY no other American city lives so close to its earth. You must think of prairie. Beyond the flatness of Lake Michigan another flatness. A thousand miles of it, rising with incalculable leisure to the sudden climax of the Rocky Mountains. This is the prairie. Rich black earth spread like the sky. The Mississippi and his legion of waters make it fecund. Nations of Indians called it their world and their mother. Buffalo roamed over it like the winds. And then the white man. Buffalo and Indians vanished. But the loam of the plains was ready like a wanton woman. Here was a race who would plant endless wheat and corn, a race of insatiate desire. The prairie would have fruit to dower and dominion the world. Here at last was a race of lovers to satisfy a prairie.

The train flows over the flat land. Green farms, the warm, brown lurch of country roads wither away. Here is a sooty sky hanging forever lower. The sun is a red ball retreating. The heave of the prairie lies palpable still to the grimed horizons. But on it, a thick deposit: gray, drab, dry—litter of broken steel, clutter of timber, heapings of brick. The sky is a stain: the air is streaked with runnings of grease and smoke. Blanketing the prairie, this fall of filth, like black snow—a storm that does not stop. . . . The

117

train glides farther in toward the storm's center. Chimneys stand over the world, and belch blackness upon it. There is no sky now. Above the bosom of the prairie, the spread of iron and wooden refuse takes on form. It huddles into rows: it rises and stampedes and points like a lay of metal splinters over a magnet. This chaos is polarized. Energy makes it rigid and direct. Behold the roads without eyes wrench into line: straighten and parallel. The endless litter of wood is standing up into wooden shanties. The endless shanties of wood assemble to streets. Iron and smoke and brick converge and are mills and yards. The shallow streets mount like long waves into a sea of habitations. And all this tide is thick above the prairie. Dirt, drab houses, dominant chimneys. A sky of soot under the earth of flaming ovens. Rising into a black crescendo as the train cuts underneath high buildings, shrieking freight-cars, to a halt. But on all sides still, with vast flanks spreading and breathing and inviting, the unburied prairie. . . .

Chicago is a symbol. A splendid one, not subtle and hidden away but brutal like itself, and naked clear. A symbol that speaks in the facts of its life. An open city. On the east, the fresh Michigan sea. Prairie everywhere else. Let it spread free like the dirty winds that tear it to bits. Even the Lake makes contribution of its mud. Widens the shores. Even the Lake—and all else to what measure!—gives of its depths to fatten Chicago.

You have come in on a train. Everywhere trains come into Chicago. In the moneyed precincts by the

Lake, in the endless wooden miles of the poor West Side, in the industrial hells to the South. A vast flat city, cut to bits by tracks of steel. A lacerated city. A city destroyed by the iron flails that beat it into being.

There is no peace in the Chicago streets. But there are freight-cars.

A mile of avenue. Low houses, soiled and blind, with garish fronts for shops, facing a clanging gutter. And then, the trolley lurches with gnashing wheel and there is a freight-yard. Myriad tracks, burdened with unloading box-cars, along which the engines scatter their black message over the city. A dim place at day with its soot and grime and the dust of the plains shedding from its iron conduits. And at night an inferno: red flame and black shadow and the loom of masses sliding on tracks through the torn city.

With the long steel thrusts of its railways, all America mangles Chicago: and by the channels of its thrusts pours produce, pours wealth, pours of its life, and makes Chicago. Freight-cars block streets, engine-smoke blinds windows. Even the water comes in upon the open city. Two rivers curl about the town like sleepy pythons. High boats from the Lake stand also above the houses. Like the roads of steel, the river-roads play havoc with the streets: cut them open, choke traffic. Masses of men black the fenders of a draw-bridge while three fat tugs laze by, piled up with onions and manure. By the river as by the tracks, the streets have their shapes and their meaning.

Warehouses stand sheer from the waters, where boats

can moor and time be saved. And on the houses' other side, the frenzy of shops and merchantmen, selling the stuff of the ships. Factories make their way close to the train-yards. The cars run their coal and their ore to the ovens' mouth. Such are the masters, hewing the city to their imperious needs. Houses where men dwell merely are shoved away, out of sight, into off-hand pools where neither rail nor river runs. For these are the true blood-conduits of Chicago. By them, the life is quickest, life's meaning clearest. Factory and mill, standing insatiate over the train yards and the rivers, speak for the city which they have gathered about them.

In the South Side, in what has become the heart of Chicago, stretch the stinking miles of stockyards. Dante would have recognized this world. A sunken city of blood. Black buildings loom over narrow, muddy paths where the sun cannot dry the slime. Fantastic chutes and passage-ways twist against the sky, leading into the shadow of muffled houses. Muffled sounds disappear against the reeking walls. Men move about with bloody hands and the whites of their eyes gleaming. Beyond, the pens of the cattle. Miles of them also. A prostrate, charted world for the towering hell. Cut through by steel-rails and snorting locomotives. And on the other side, the pens of the men and women who slay the cattle and who, in turn, are consumed.

Less regular, these pens of men. Streets? Scarcely. Rather alleys that limp through puddles and broken gutters to other alleys—or into refuse piles—or into walls. Low, sodden houses of wood. Windows tight shut in summer, in order to keep out the thickest of the stench. Acid-eaten, soot-stained houses, soaked with all the floating excrement of the meat-mills. In them at night, Slav and Magyar and Croat who dreamed of a Promised Land. And at day, children playing in the filth of the streets, waiting to grow up, waiting to join their parents.

On the one side, trains pour in the cattle and the hogs. On the other, trains pour in the men and the women. Cattle and hogs from the West. Women and men from the East. Between, stockaded off by the dripping walls, the slaughter-houses stand mysterious, and throb to their ceaseless profit. High buildings over a sunken world, knitted together by elevated rails and secret compacts. Knitted into a sort of hierarchy whose sort of power is manifest about them. But over all, and joining all, over the meat and the men and the feudal masters, is something else. The spirit of the place—perhaps its soul: an indescribable stench. It is composed of mangled meat, crushed bone, blood soaking the floors, corroding the steel, and sweat. A stench that is warm and thick, and that is stubborn. A stench somehow sorrowful and pregnant, as if the sweat of men joined with the guts of beasts brought forth a new drear life. And when the wind is from the south, this stench is wafted out to the entire city.

Chicago is the dream of the industrial god. Chaos incarnate.

The miracle of Chicago is that it is also something

else. The miracle of Chicago is that this stew of steel and smoke should be inhabited by men and women.

Looking upon Chicago, you might see no miracle. Here is a sticky smudge on the face of the prairie. Alive it must be with maggots and with midges. Makers of soot: eaters of soot: dwellers in iron. Not men and women. So the observer might have it. The poet has only his dream. . . .

Go into the Chicago streets. The elevated trains make greater noise, the street cars are more brutal tangents of commotion, than in the Eastern cities. The murky coating over the sky shuts in the fever of life, raises it to a higher, stifled power. But though the city reaches up in stone, or flattens to an unending desert of wood dwellings, there is an unbridled force about, that is not these things.

The Chicagoan is alive. He is not cowed: he is not refined away: there is a part of him still which the Machine has not sucked nor the black air blighted. The Chicagoan walks with swift step through the harshness of his city. But his feet are somehow planted on the prairie. His feet have not forgotten the feel of the rich loam: nor the greenness which comes forth from it.

Do not talk to the Chicagoan! He will talk business. He will talk size. He will talk ugly. He will boast of the steel-straitjacket which has not yet quite girthed him. He will compare his mills and railroads with the cash of New York. He does not know what he is saying. He does not know that he is still alive. He is like a young free man, with happy gait, aping the authoritative stiffness of his Papa. This life in him is all unuttered: and he is pouring it fast into a mold that must destroy it. Only the hell in which he somehow has survived speaks and knows its meaning. He gives his life to the furtherance of that death. He rushes like a poet through the streets. But it is to serve the Mills.

Therefore, if Chicago is the city of Hope, the reason is that there, Despair has simply not yet altogether won. Chicago is still fluent, still chaotic. In the black industrial cloak are still interstices of light.

New York has *set*. New York is so perfectly Industrialism's flower, that no flower is left. Industrial disorder has its order. Industrial anarchy has its law. New York is clutched in them. But in Chicago, the chaos is still chaos. The material is still raw, and therefore pregnant. In many ways, this turbulent city represents to-day what New York was years ago. It is unkempt, uncouth, ceremonious and callous. It has little inkling of Metropolitan behavior. It is not organized. It lacks coördination. It is not altogether and irrevocably pledged. New York was once like this, but with a difference. Thirty years ago, Industrialism was still hale and absolute in its blighting sway. It held New York in a grip that no other force contested, no vision in America could swerve. New York was doomed. To-day, Chicago moves in the same course, is driven by the same control. But during these thirty years Industrialism has grown weaker, Puritanism paler. They have proved their failure to supply the loves and the desires of already one non-pioneering generation. A new Order raises its rebel head and looks about for itself. A new vision disputes the encompassing blindness.

Another thirty years like the thirty that have passed, and the Miracle would live no more in the Chicago streets. It would be dead. The prairie would be buried under the smoke and the steel and the stench. The men who walk would not feel the loam beneath their feet: the touch of creative life would be gone from their blood. They would be altogether bound by the dead world they gave their lives to build. But another thirty years like the thirty that have passed——?

. . . .

In order that there might live our Hope against such a future, an American generation has been given up to hopelessness.

These are the men whom the old gods abandoned. They were children of the myths upon which America was built. They believed in the perfection of their country, in the infallibility of the Constitution. America was "the land of the free and home of the brave." Justice, happiness, the highest of ideals were the very stuff of American life. These men believed also in the righteousness of American ways. Morality, as the churches defined it, was absolute. It was inclusive of all possible good: it was exclusive of all possible harm.. American society was the best conceivable, quite like American government. Also, they believed in church religion. The pioneer replica of Christ was not pale, not unreal to them. He was God; the pat ways he

124

taught were godly. And outside the pale of these ways and these professions was heathen Hell.

Then, with the industrial buccaneering that followed the Civil War, and with the damaging revelations of Charles Darwin, their whole structure of contentment vanished. These men found themselves no longer believers in a moralistic God. Looking behind their fallen Idol, they found that Puritanism had hidden a festering mass of hideous repression. They found ugliness and sterility and disease playing beneath the white complexion of the moralists. So they no longer believed in morals. But they discovered more. The pillars of their church screwed money out of prostrate debtors; the lawyers who delivered the Fourth-of-July orations "lobbied" the Legislatures and got rich on graft; the editors who preached the impeccability of the Constitution were in the pay of the Trusts. These men began to be suspicious of American laws: of the American Government. And soon their keen eyes showed them that the "land of the brave" was in fact a land of greedy and unscrupulous exploiters, since they owned most of it; and that the "home of the free" was fast becoming a people of economic serfs.

With sure fingers, these undeluded men went over the fabric of Puritan America and found it rotting, and found it full of lies. So they cast their old gods from them, under whose benison these lies had thriven. Godless, they faced the world.

Children they were after all of Material America. And now, their searching minds had taught them the emptiness of the material world. And only emptiness was left. For they had knowledge for thrusting out false gods, reviling a hideous material reality. But they had no faith to create new worlds, new gods to live with.

A whole generation that was still the child of the world which it denied. What of desire, of love, of creativity these men possessed was bound by the old ties to the old gods and myths. And when their proud minds forced them to cast out these gods and myths—cut these ties—what of desire and love they had went from them also. They remained stranded upon Disillusion.

They know, these men, only that nothing can be known. They love only what their conviction tells them is not: tells them to deny. So that they love only their denial. They face a world they have helped clear of aged falsehood. But, desireless save in what they have destroyed, they are material-bound quite like the world they have struck clear of:—more, since that world had its old gods and myths, however tottering; and they have none. In the emptiness of their convictions, they can only freeze and starve.

And yet, they are a generation which has found passionate voice. The price of their liberation has been Despair. But even that despair was an adventure: to it they brought the quickening of their life. Despair moves forth, sweeping the cluttered lies from the American consciousness, to-day. And in so far prepares the hope of Our America. . . .

Edgar Lee Masters still practices law in Chicago. Like the typical Chicagoan, he came to the city from the soil. A town called Garnet in Kansas where he was born in 1868, and another called Lewiston in Illinois where he first practiced law, served him for background. He is an angular, hard-muscled, big-domed man. He wears ungainly clothes and an ugly derby hat, hiding his brow. His teeth show that he has recently chewed tobacco. A serious, plodding, passionate man, this Masters: friend of Labor, graduate democrat and radical, student of ancient pessimisms. A fellow with the clutched lips of the fighter for bread, and with the tender eyes of a child. For many years he went to law in the Chicago courts, often taking his stand against the windmills of Plutocracy, and wrote plays, poems, political essays of the sort that might have been expected. Polished verse, rich in classical allusion, perfect in classical form. The verse of the Voltairian grasping for culture beyond the Chicago smoke: verse having nothing much to do with either Masters or Chicago. And then, in a year of anguish, Masters forgot about rimes and reached for the wound in his own heart. *The Spoon River Anthology* came into the world.

The citizens of a Western town speak the secret of their lives from the graveyard where they have been buried. Bare, clear statements they are, in verse that more or less adheres to the blank pentameter. Ironical and tragic. An occasional burst of lyric asseveration. Many of the utterances sharp like acid, epigrams of the heart. No voices raised. Many are mere dim whispers, dealing with lurid tragedy obliquely, as blood might seep through a thick soil. And so, voice after

127

voice, the gradual polyphony is woven. A Western village, hidden beneath the pretty garb of Puritan convention, festering, lusting, murderous. The simple device of the poet in letting the *buried* speak is one of those unwitting harmonies of form and spirit and classical instruction that proclaim the genius. The whole burden of Masters' song is of the burial of love and life beneath the crass deposits of the American world. His community is common with all others in that love dwells in it, and aspiration and the need of beauty and the dream of human service. But all is thwarted. Love becomes lust and poison and despair: aspiration turns acid and devours: souls starve, women kill, dreams blight. The silence of convention, the scared cruelty of the driven herd, the Baal of success have done these things: have buried these loving men and women. Now they speak from the grave. And it is marvelous how cavernous and distant and serene become their voices with their many-sided burdens of deprivation.

The *Anthology* is not great poetry. It has no wings. It is eyeless. But it is a great book, precisely because it is so noble an expression of the winglessness and eyelessness of him who wrote it: and of the generation whose voice he is. Of course, the pretension of certain critics is *naif* that the *Anthology* is a *Comédie humaine,* a novel in abbreviated verse. Nothing of the sort. It is a strictly lyrical expression. It does not create in three-dimensioned form the multiple life of our American town. Very few of these buried, suffering creatures achieve that dynamic unity which the novelistic and dramatic arts require. But all of them

most poignantly create the impression which that life
has made upon the poet: are stops by means of which
he variates his theme. And that theme is the Despair
of all his middle-generation, the cry, part anguished
and part wistful, of those who have lost old gods and
found no new ones.

Perhaps the most majestic monument of this transition by which America needed to journey upward into
birth is in the novels of Theodore Dreiser. Dreiser
belongs to the same world as Masters. He was born
in Terre Haute, a provincial city of Indiana, in 1871.
There is Catholic German blood in his veins. Unlike
Masters he has professionally followed writing all his
life, and has come East to New York. And yet, deeply,
the two are brothers. And deeply, they express a
muffled music of which Chicago is the tonal key.

Dreiser is the creator of a hero. Dreiser is a genius
of epic reach, even if not of epic texture. In some
ways, he is more the typical Western Yankee even than
his friend. He is a big man, ambling of gait, loose-
armed and gentle-footed. His slow voice rises with the
love of argument. He is cantankerous, sensitive, sentimental. A burly giant with a face as tender as a little
girl's. A body full of vast desire and a face in love
with sweetness. In the disharmony of this, a great
grief writ upon his face, and a stern anguish drenching
his works.

The hero of Dreiser is the multi-millionaire. He has
taken the complacent *picaro* of the Broadway Play, the
child-hero of Horatio Alger's "From Rags to Riches,"
and reduced him to the spiritual penury that must be

his lot in a world full of gold and joyless, pent with activity and void of *being*. This great period of American life—the period which now awakes to the bankruptcy of pioneering—Dreiser has forevermore expressed.

But, like Masters, expressed unconsciously. Masters thought he was depicting life—all life—in his American town. And in reality he portrayed the spiritual dearth of his own outlook. Something was lacking, something that lived in Spoon River but not in Masters. Thus also, Dreiser paints the splendors of a man of might—Titan or Genius—and in sooth pens the confessional of his own failure to find true values of existence in the American world about him.

But the failure leads to an artistic triumph. Out of this spiritual void, Dreiser creates æsthetic *form*. For this inner lack of being, whose unconscious medium he is, is universal; is the pioneer's. This he has fixed and rendered memorable.

The stuff of Dreiser's novels corresponds with amazing clearness to the stuff of our American life. It is unlit and undifferentiated. His books have the crude form of simple massiveness. Some elemental force like Gravity holds them together and propels them. They are not integrated. The artist who is aware of the values of being touches his materials with that awareness and makes them live. Each element of his work will glow with an inner fire, quite as each quality of being is a flame. Such luminosity you will not find in Dreiser. Nor in America. His books move. But they move like herds.

And yet, they are vital. They lack characterization; often they seem, while one is plowing through them, mere heaped obstructions of reiterated incident. But when one has drawn away from them, one senses their slow, organic movement. They have a rhythm, huge, partaking of the Whole, like the rhythm of a glacier. The rhythm of inchoate, undifferentiated life. It is in this virtue that they are most like the American world.

Dreiser's principal hero, Frank Cowperwood, is like Dreiser's books and like his land. He does not seem to grow. He is not organic to that extent. Rather, he *accumulates*. He does not progress. He merely stirs. He is a reservoir of power, without synthesis of choice. He has one woman after another. They leave no deposit of experience upon his soul. He fails: he goes to prison: he marries and triumphs and fails again. He never changes. For experience alone can change. And experience is precisely what he never reaches. He is like a molecule of matter that moves unaltered through eternity. Combining now with this being, now with that: but still the irrepressible and inalterable unit.

At the end of the excursions of his heroes, the sense of Emptiness weighs upon Dreiser. And, like Masters, he transfers this sense upon the world. Many of his novels end with metaphysical abstractions: protests of life against this void of being. The truth is, that lacking the virtue of experience, the measure of subjective being, Dreiser, filling his books with incident and facts, fills them only with symbols of vacuity. His Genius, Eugene Witla, goes through the welter of the world like a runner through a haystack. Come out at the other end, he shakes himself and looks at the daughter whom accident has somehow dropped into his hands, with a creeping sense of unreality. Witla has been a famous painter, a king of the publishing world, a failure, a laborer, a lover. But he has never for a moment created life out of the kaleidoscope of these occurrings. He has done everything: *been* not at all. No wonder he looks up at the stars like a lost lamb and unconsciously pleads for the warm flock.

In this longing, the Genius betrays the author. Dreiser, deep in his soul, yearns for the gods he has flung away: for the sweet comfort of a myth. If his Desire could face the actual world, it would soon warm it and make it glow. And since it does not, the cause can only be that it is facing elsewhere. Like the generation which he best expresses, Theodore Dreiser has cut away from the tradition and worship of the American past, only at the expense of the emotional energy which made that tradition and that worship live. The stuff of his books is not in flame, because the fire of his own soul is not free to ignite it. He is still caught in his own past.

From this circumstance, moreover, we may understand why Dreiser and Masters and their brothers spend such vehemence in attack upon the Past from which they should be free. They are not free. They attack because the Past is still so emotionally real; because it holds them back from full bestowal upon the Present. The man whose life pours uninhibited into the world about him is too busy creating to attack. We attack only what hinders and holds. The protest of

132

Dreiser against American ghosts shows how fearfully America is still haunted by them. Masters' absorption in classical forms and classical allusions, Dreiser's rapt interest in the scientific formulæ which twenty years ago seemed to promise a substitute for the vision of Genesis, point to their ancient yearnings.

The Past is still with us in this land. At best, the Present is a feeble growth. Dreiser and Masters mark the transition of revolt. They have denied the old gods. But we shall not be free of the old, till we have found the new.

.   .   .   .

Neighbors of these valiant and hindered warriors there are, who have pushed nearer to the present, lost more fear of the disabling past. A newer generation: still struggling, still bleeding, still, let us admit it, weak. But not without the valor of their hope.

I think at once of Sandburg.

Carl Sandburg's father was a Swede named August Johnson. There were too many Johnsons in the construction-gang of the Western railroad where he worked. So this Johnson changed his name. Carl was born in the town of Galesburg, Illinois, just ten years later than Masters in Kansas. He drove a milkwagon, pitched wheat, washed dishes: he was a soldier in the Philippines. He went back to Galesburg and to college. Then, he became a labor editor on a Milwaukee journal, secretary to Milwaukee's socialist mayor. Finally, a year after the appearance of *Spoon River*, he brought out his *Chicago Poems*. Masters wrote a generous foreword. But the difference in texture of these two volumes is like the difference between night and dawn. Night is perhaps more solid: surer of itself. It is less the wavering evanescent thing that steals like dim thought across the breaking skies. Night is an Empire. Dawn is an outpost.

Sandburg singing:

"I speak of new cities and new people.
I tell you the past is a bucket of ashes.
I tell you yesterday is a wind gone down, a sun dropping in the west.
I tell you there is nothing in the world only an ocean of to-morrows, a sky of to-morrows.
I am a brother of the cornhuskers who say at sundown: To-morrow is a day."

What has he found in his prairies? Pitchforks, biscuits, coffee, harvest and rivetters, coonskin caps and Omaha and smoke, shanties and hogs and skyscrapers and grain. What has he found in his Chicago? Laborers pale at the morning whistle, booze and hovels and whores, shop-girls with slack breasts, icemen with bloody eyes. Nothing of the new cities, nothing of the new people about these. This prairie and this Chicago stink already with the age of sterile adventure. Something new this Sandburg must have found, to make him sing like a dawn. . . . He has found himself.

He comes of this ravening ugly world. He is of it. Yet, he lives. And he has found that he lives. There is this rapture in his song.

You cannot mistake it. That is the new god: that is the to-morrow he is so full of. Nothing but this amazing revelation—all in that—that he is alive. O you Europeans who have lived so long, who have high cathedrals and ancient words for monuments to life, you do not know what ecstasy it is when an American discovers that he lives!

That cry is not very strong, but it is very wise. Behind it, the deep silences of death and of denial. Making its volume, but a frail outset of the flesh. But do not mistake it. It is a birth-cry.

Carl Sandburg walks through the same desert with Masters and with Dreiser. On all sides, penury of desire, on all sides the clamped dominion of Puritan and Machine. A desert of mangled dreams. But there is Sandburg walking through it also. Quite as real as this shallow eye fixed on the stock-lists, as that hank of hair selling you crockery in the basement. So it cannot be quite a desert after all.

Carl Sandburg is aware of himself: that means aware of life: that means in love. Now watch what happens to his words. They are luminous—always of course the best of them, for sometimes Sandburg forgets and gets mad and begins writing propaganda. They have form. Strong, tender shoots of verse, exquisite, perfect, pushing up through the filth like grass upon the prairie. Lines just so clear and succulent and green. Direction just so dynamically upward. In the first book, the level of the grass is still lost in the refuse scattering his plain. In the second book *(Cornhuskers)* the blades are clearer and higher. A true poet—and living a true life. A lover of this crass world, and by his love a distiller of its beauty.

Do not expect too much quite yet. These miracles are slow. . . . But here is water. Here is the eternal seed. Life needs no more. Something is indeed pushing high from the black loam of the prairie. High through the smudge and the steel. Higher. They have not prevailed, with their magnificent night!

For Sandburg has comrades. Sherwood Anderson for one.*

The Chicago "trade" will tell you of an advertising fellow by that name. He writes "copy" for bright brands of axle-grease, steel-plows and harness. He "sits in" with the directors of country canneries and tells them how they can boost their output of tomatoes. He makes alluring texts for anything from suspenders to pianolas. And the "trade" will tell you that, in addition—so they say—this Anderson makes stories. "In his spare time." When he runs up to Michigan or down to Kansas to plan the campaign of a local buggy-manufacturer, he takes a pad with him. Seated beside some salesman in the smoker, he finishes a chapter begun perhaps a month before in his last spare hour. Nights, he shakes off the grime of business, he seeks himself in the stillness of his room: he lights a candle to his secret gods: he pulls out the mussed pad from his coat and writes some more.

Once, Anderson was a laborer. Then, he was a soldier in the Spanish War. Then a small Lutheran College, called Wittenberg, in his native state Ohio, gave him six months' education. At last, he hauled himself up by his own boot-straps and became a busi-

* Born at Camden, Ohio, in 1876.

ness man. A good business man he was. Full of ideas, sparkling with witty measures. And he made money. His mind slithered about the dull deliberations of country bankers, of promoters from the cities. His will fuelled them and dazzled them and made them bob about as if he had their purses on a string. There was the making of a regular millionaire in Sherwood Anderson. He was on the way—the highway. But unfortunately something happened.

What happened to Sherwood Anderson and turned him from the traveled American road of making-money is of a vast significance: not as regards the life of Anderson alone, but in the life of the United States. It was this: He found in himself two growing senses: the sense of boredom and the sense of dirt. Think of that! Money in his hand. Country bankers dancing before him with their treasured loans. And then, this unseemly, this un-American mood in Anderson, turning him away.

A sense of shame. Anderson felt sorry for his financiers. He understood them. He felt sorry for the men and women who produced for them and made their money. He understood them also. It is hard to do good business with a man you understand. It would be sweeter, somehow, to talk with him, to play with him, to help him. It would be cleaner to live with him, than to trick him down. Anderson found that money-making was a tedious routine. What did it bring him after all? One narrowed down the rich processes of one's mind to the monomania of acquisition. One brushed aside life and thought. One lied, one tricked, one harped at a miserable game: and at the end had nothing but the narrowness to which one had perforce been cramping down one's life.

So Anderson was thirty-five; and clever and shrewd and strong. But a great boredom weighed upon his soul. And it seemed to him that he was breathing, walking through, an unclean world.

Anderson began to write. He stopped meeting his fellows so regularly, evenings, at the café. He withdrew to his room, and began talking to himself. He came of a world in which art was a distant mystery. The artist was a "special kind of guy." *He* was a business-man. But he guessed even the business-man had a right, if he was prematurely old and sick at heart, to hide in a room and maunder to himself. He needed an escape from the binding ugliness about him. He sought himself. He made a world of what he found. He wrote his first story, as five hundred years ago his forebears might have gone to Church and to confession. But there were no Cathedrals in Anderson's Middle-west. Churches aplenty, but all given up, more or less, to the hard ugliness he needed to escape. He made his own confessional.

Thus, his first novel was written. He put it in a trunk. He was still a business man. There was no way out from that. But somehow, he was already not the same. His lavish energy, bursting in wit and fertile vision, had played about his business affairs. Now most of that energy was elsewhere. He had been restless, miserable, reckless because his energy had had no work worthy his measure. Unconsciously, now, he settled down. Business bored him less, now that he no longer let it run him. Business became a master, only if one desired to master it. His normal American will to become rich had left him like a fever gone with the new Spring. He did not know why he no longer wanted to be rich: why he was suddenly content to plod along with a good day's pay. But the reason was clear enough. Such work made no great demands upon the deeper and higher sources of his being which now he could pour elsewhere. Such work, he could do with his fingers, and let his heart do other.

So the rich man died, and slowly from his sacrifice the artist rose.

Anderson wrote another novel and put it in his trunk. And a third and a fourth. One night he walked the Chicago streets till dawn. Tears were in his eyes, his heart bounded in his throat, fever ran through his veins. He had read over what he had written. It had come to him that it was beautiful. "I am an artist! I am an artist!" he said, blinded with revelation.

And so, a new care crept into his secret work. He learned respect for the written word: he learned to venerate the truth that gushed like a hidden spring from his pent life. He wrote more religiously. He went out into the world where he did penance for his bread with a new seeking consciousness. For he had learned that the world of his secret hours was after all the same as the one in which he worked. A world infinitely serious. He had found an escape, not from it, but from its superficial lies. Relief lay in the truth: in bringing it forth from life: in endowing it with form.

A world he needed to create in order to feel clean. But since in the reality about him, the ruck and the dross, the refuse and the unborn clogged in unending chaos, let him bring clarity to it and form. He needed to find the cleanliness of revelation against the dirty counterfeit in which he trafficked. For many years he had earned his way through a world where cant and subterfuge and greed covered life, dimmed its colors, stopped its throb. But he knew through the fact that something in him yearned, that something in him loved, how underneath some loveliness must persist. Let him cut under and find out.

One day this author of many stories met a real writer. It was a wonderful experience for Anderson, a still greater one for Dell. Floyd Dell was the literary critic of a Chicago paper. They talked. Anderson let slip his secret. Dell read the manuscript of the first book and took it shouting to New York. Publishers saw it and turned away. Then Dell in a flash of intuition sent the novel to England. An English house cabled to its New York office to sign a contract for three volumes. So at last, Anderson was published.

That first work, *Windy McPherson's Son*, is significant only in that it traces the design of Anderson's own growth. Theodore Dreiser had written the epic novel of the millionaire. A man helpless like a child with the gleaming bauble of gold which had been dropped into his lap. Helpless and wanton and ignorant too far, to find even real joy of it. In Anderson's book, the hero follows the American myth. He also leaves his country town where he sold papers, grows rich, marries the daughter of his employer, and supersedes him. That is the first portion of the book—whose full development one finds far more fertilely in Dreiser. At this juncture, however, Anderson's man discovers he is empty, hungry and unclean. He wanders off from his vast wealth! A ridiculous adventure for an American magnate. He "chucks his job" literally as Anderson figuratively his. And he takes the road.

The tale of McPherson's Odyssey is weak and fleshless. It is important as a pattern. And a pattern not alone of Anderson's revolt, but of the slow turning in the American world. For what McPherson did futilely and Anderson in person, America must fulfill in her social and spiritual life. She has come to the climax of material wealth. She must discover that she is empty, that she is hungry and unclean. She must learn, to the last bitter lesson, the sterility and falsehood of her Puritan, possessive world. She must go forth, and she must go within, to create her own salvation.

So it came about that this harassed small-town promoter of the Middle-west, sick with a creeping and unnamed disaffection, slunk away from his associates and in the silence of his room wrote a simple, half-trivial tale that is a Prophecy for the American world.

Since then, the prophet has matured as artist.

In all of Anderson's work, the element of escape is clear. He is a man imprisoned, caught up inextricably through economic needs in the industrial disorder. Through his art he seeks release. This is evident in the simplicity, the fanciful directness of his style. He is a man, after the close of a shrieking day, who seeks a quiet music.

It is natural, therefore, that Anderson should have gone back to the town of his childhood and made of it and its associations his finest instrument. The heroine of his life is his mother. He is too strong a man to evade truth in his search for spiritual satisfaction, to concoct minor fantasies and live in them. But in his past is a reality strong and true and pure: the reality of his mother. And when Anderson goes to her he strikes an equal note. It seems that she was a woman marvelously clear in her intuitions and brave in love. Poverty and worse crushed her early. Anderson tells his friends the story of her loneliness through life: of her uncompanioned toil: of the many children and the town that seemed to take no notice. He tells the amazement of them all when, at his mother's death, the whole village followed bareheaded to the grave. The neighbors had been too harried themselves to see her much, to help her any, during her life. And yet she had gone forth, somehow, the spirit of her silence, and filled the village. One feels that Anderson's mystical knowledge of the Middle western town came of this love, and went with it, partaking of its conquest.

For if this town belongs to Anderson's own past, he has flushed it with a consciousness of life and love which must create for us the America of our to-morrow. He calls it Winesburg. He has written many stories about it. Simple tales, often mere anecdotes of this character and that. Yet drawn, for the most part, with a curve and a line that reveal infinite distance.

There is something magical about these stories. The magic of life, perhaps. One looks into the eyes of a woman and one feels there the vistas of being: great spaces filled with sense and the mists where sense is drowned. One can find no word for this. The eyes are a form. One knows their physiology. One can never know how cups so frail and slight should hold so measureless a measure. The best tales of Anderson are like this. The recital of an afternoon, or love on a hill at dusk, or gossip of men on Main Street. But he has poured into his words a sense of life that is immeasurable. This sense, however, is inseparable from the story quite as their sight is inseparable from eyes. One may say that vision and eyes are different things. One may puzzle over the disparate value of these simple tales and the vision they unfold. But one cannot sever. In other words, Anderson's stories have true æsthetic form. They are material impregnate. In them is that impalpable marriage of substance and of human spirit which is art.

Winesburg embraces America. The stifled restless present buried in its past: and thrust forth from it a blind and magnificent desire. So young McPherson seeking wealth in the City and turning his back upon it: so young George Willard, dizzy in the clouds of his misgivings: so Beaut McGregor, the unconscious poet, stirred by the social rhythm of his day to express the pathos of his longing in the barbaric "tom-tom" measure of *Marching Men.* . . . So, finally, Anderson himself, seeking health and sanity—as must all his people —in the elemental let of self-expression.

The Spoon River Anthology marks the effect of our life-denying life: sin and disease and death. You will find them no less in *Winesburg*. But you will also find, impregnate in its words, the impulses of life. Impulses which, in their material obsession, made for the denial of impulse, tended toward death: but at their source were no less living, and after their release from the tyranny of the American perversion, shall live again. This one finds in *Winesburg*: the conflict of American life against its own rigid forms, the new upward-stirring, the fierce passion of renewal. *Spoon River* is static: *Winesburg* is dynamic. *Spoon River* is the trampled and buried face of the American world: *Winesburg* is its heart.

. . . .

One more who must be mentioned. Frederick Booth in a slightly different way has taken his stand against the momentum of our past: gives us another vision of lonely men, walking windy streets, performing dusty tasks—nursing a dream.

Booth was born on a farm near Nobelsville, Indiana, a little later than Anderson and Sandburg—in 1882. Like them, he came to Chicago—the pattern path of desiring Western youth. But an added touch of sophistication left him dissatisfied, and in 1907 he struck eastward to New York.

He had his bag full of short-stories. Sending them forth, he met the traditional repulse. Booth is one of those unfortunate elect who desire to do nothing but create. His stories brought him no bread. He went back to Indiana and for three more years he was a farmhand and a carpenter. But finally, he returned to New York. He has stayed there, writing, ever since.

The outline of this career is usual enough. But the usual goes no deeper. Most writers strike a compromise—often unconscious—with the easy editors. Those writers who cannot, and who need to earn their bread, do something else to earn it. Booth knew no compromise, and he needed bread. He kept on writing, even at times when he did not keep on eating. He retired to a little room. His assault on the magazines abated. It has become a siege. Occasionally, some cheap periodical will print one of his stories whose clear perfection seems to shriek against the gray and muddy pages. Very rarely some radical magazine bears his name. Never by any chance an organ of the sort that pays a living price. Mere skirmishes, these: interludes of siege. Booth remains unknown, and his work remains unprinted. He stays in his bare room and works, and eats when he can. And in the anguished vigil of his condition, he brings his share to the American expression.

A slender and frail and stooping figure. A brow that is over-heavy with pensive travail. Eyes full of a pity that is simply vision. Booth is priest of the new American gods. Anderson and Sandburg stride into the smoke to battle. Booth prays. Anderson's broad arm strikes with success for the sweet Mystery of Failure. Booth lives it. These are new gods that have as yet few lovers. Their priest must live the sorrowful passion of their disregarded truth. As the early Christian dwelt aside, seeking pain to fortify his

prayer, so Booth, living upon the solitude and the indifference of his world.

Booth is the most conscious of our vital prose artists.
The herd lyrism of Dreiser, the personal lyrism of Anderson are lacking in his purely objective art. His
prose stands away like sculpture, moves of itself like
music. He is an obsessed observer of the human fact:
this brings to his work a striking clarity of surface
that recalls Flaubert. But he is primarily the mystic.
His mastery of the objective world becomes the servant
of his individual interpretation. He uses the passion
and the manner of American life as words to sing a
song of his own. With him, in consequence, the materials of the American world take on the sanctity of
his own devotion: the impulse of the artist becomes
religious seed to impregnate America.

. . . .

Now, these three men are American: in each detail
they share and make the typical American experience.
This is not their value: this is what they hold with
many million others. What counts is their conduit to
the average mass, and the spark of fire which they can
therefore bring to it.

By means of them—and of their like for they are
but outstanding among others—we find within our
land the one thing needed, the one thing missed: inherent life. All of their purpose is to disclose the luminosity of American materials. Against the American
doctrine of success with its subsidiary Puritan morale,
they bring their gospel of Failure. Meaning only this:
that the material ends to which we have reduced the

largess of our lives are shoddy falsehood, and that the glory of truth is but the glory of *being*. An ancient gospel that gleams with the fierceness of its need in the American night.

Such then, the miracle of Chicago. The industrial Despair is still loose enough and weak in the Middle-west so that such truths as these could push up into some sort of light. These spirits are facts. They cannot be ignored. And cannot be destroyed. They create values out of the American chaos. They show that men may still meet their city and their prairie, and have life of them. With them, new gods come out of the corn: and shoulder their way across the iron streets.

VI. THE PURITAN SAYS "YEA"

New England is a tragedy of ambition. Other lands have been more isolate. Other people equally inbred. Doubtless, the furious extremes of the New England climate are worsted elsewhere. But surely in no place has a riding and obsessive will collaborated so with Nature to drive a prosperous community upon death. The New Englander, one feels, might have endured the inclemency of his landside: he has succumbed to the inclemency of his mind.

The Puritan loves to be in the minority. Only in that condition can he assert his pride of power. And he is in the minority even at home. In Massachusetts and Connecticut, the two most populous New England States, two-thirds of the people are of foreign parentage or birth. Celts, Latins, Jews swarm the industrial centers and the farms of this ancient country. The Puritan is driven farther upon his rocky soil, deeper into his austere self. And still, he rules. He has not flung his dominion over the continent to lose it in the corner where it was born. Let Boston speak Italian, the quiet accent of Harvard will still tell it what to say. Let Lowell and Lawrence and other of the innumerable milltowns of Massachusetts pullulate with Slav and Magyar, the guidance still comes from State Street, the wealth goes there—the same State Street which was the mother of the American Revolution. Newspaper, Church, Banking-house and Senate are Puritan. And whatever voices rise from New England show the presence of alien tongues only in their harsh resistance.

Yet no one will deny, despite his power, that the Puritan is sick. His voice is clear but it is shrill. He holds on hard, but with muscles tensioned by the approach of death. He has his face set firm against the Sun; and he glories in the cold that courses through his veins.

For more than three hundred years, he has wilfully slain life for power. And from the material of his race, mastery has sprung. But also, from the material of his race, life has been drained away. Too many generations of denying it. These gaunt men have been whittled down from the lusty Englishman. The fat is gone from their throats and they speak nasally. These dry women are children of the ruddy girl of Yorkshire. They preside in the New England homes: it is they who must bring the nearness of beauty and love to their menfolk and their babes. The Puritan has won his kingdom: now he banquets with a ghost.

The Kingdom is America, perhaps. But the ghost dwells in the New England farm. A drooping generation, godless yet stomachless: without any joy beyond the dogged cultivation of self-pain. Insanity is common. Neurosis is birthright. Life, downed by precept, has become a hidden thing that gnaws and festers. It cannot die. It was denied when it was hearty and flung visions of joy and play against the business of wealth. It must be denied now more than ever when it has become a cancer running against the gray rhythm of Puritan existence. For the will has prevailed. Therein lies the beautiful logic of New England. There is indeed no heaven left on earth to waste attention. No aspiration beyond the immediate object. No enterprise in men beyond the grasping of their hands. No loveliness in women beyond the bare business of their sex. A people stripped indeed for material possession. A people stripped, in consequence, even of the capacity to enjoy it. Men who cultivate alone the soil soon lose the sun that makes it fecund. . . .

Thus New England, in its typical conclusion. It denied life in its sweet tangents of desire, in order to have the power it desired. And now its desire is without eyes: and its life is a hidden, shameful thing.

But there is no death, even as there is no black in Nature. New England is a tragedy, not because she has destroyed herself, but because she is capable of salvation.

Already in the dark days before the Civil War, there was light. New England, meeting the rival greed of the South on its lowest terms, gathered the strength that was to make her victor. Industrialism was a new furnace in which the Puritan with his rapt obsession prepared to fling his life for fuel. And now a great protest, upon the level of reality, rose from New England.

Henry David Thoreau * personified this early

* Thoreau was born in Concord, Massachusetts, in 1817 and died there in 1862. His paternal great-grandparents were French people from the Isle of Guernsey. A Puritan no less for this dissenting seed.

protest. And its isolation is to be observed in the comparative obscurity of this first great American writer. Emerson was already king. And when Thoreau died, Emerson did the honors, in the *Atlantic Monthly*, for his fellow "transcendentalist" (so Thoreau called himself). And from the strictures of his praise, Thoreau is but recovering to-day.

Said Emerson: "Instead of engineering for all America, he was the captain of a huckleberry party. Pounding beans is good to the end of pounding empires, one of these days; but if, at the end of years, it is still only beans!" I suspect that Emerson must have sensed that Thoreau was in reality no transcendentalist at all: and that this was what he meant. Emerson's plan was really to leave the beans alone, and flank the empires he speaks of by the air. He reached the air, but he never laddered down to the empires. They went their materialistic ways, and, in moments of relaxation, looked up from their jobs and smiled at Emerson. Thoreau pounded beans. And to-day revolting America—young America which fights for the sanctity of life—reaches for sustenance to him. The words of Emerson who flanked empires by air-route are become vague and impalpable and abstract: the words of Thoreau who faced reality, who seceded from Massachusetts and refused to pay taxes to a State of whose deeds he could not approve, ring solid and full of virile beauty. Emerson wrote pleasant sentences over the dead body of Thoreau. But Thoreau's sentences are helping to bury Emerson to-day.

When we were boys, we all had tedious uncles who

professed to be very fond of Thoreau. They said that
Thoreau was a great naturalist; that he wrote delightfully of butterflies and mushrooms. These uncles were
typical good citizens of old America: altogether dull—
mindless and sober paragons. We decided that their
favorite author could be no favorite of ours. We took
it for granted that Thoreau also was a stuffy bore.
We left him alone. Thoreau was killed by his good
name.

It is time, however, that we wake up to the wicked,
destructive fellow Thoreau really was: give him the
bad name that is his due. For Thoreau was no naturalist at all. In his life and works, he gave expression
to the fate and hope—to the tragedy of New England.

What Rousseau was to the French, what Tolstoi was
to Russia, Thoreau was to New England. His land
stands clear against these other lands in the compari-
son. Like Rousseau, Thoreau sought a cure for the
falsehood of modern life in a return to Nature: sought
rather, by that means, a return to Self where the truth
is ever. Like Tolstoi, he was an anarchist: at war
with the privilege and ascendency of the Group over
the individual conscience. But Thoreau lacked the
fertile and mellow culture of the French which enriched
the protest of Rousseau and made it positive: he lacked
the deep mystical experience of Russia that filled out
Tolstoi's message and gave it life to move across the
world. Thoreau remained stark and naked; unadorned
like a leafless tree. In his cry against New England
he remained New England.

Through this nativity, Thoreau achieves importance

for us, even as these other men for those other, mellower peoples. He was born in New England and there he died. Boston was his Capital. His people were his neighbors. Their problems were his problems. The woods and rivers that bounded them made up his world. Whatever beauty, whatever vision he won from life, he won from New England. Thoreau had all the colloquial and intimate marks of a sectional hero. America is not so rich in such that we can afford to overlook him.

His life and his literary work are a whole so simple, so harmonious-strong, that any eager American mind may take him in. He is the great *ingénu* of our land. Lincoln is complex and dark beside him; Whitman is the product of a far more muddied world. For this very reason, Thoreau grows to-day in our need. Homogeneous America had no thirst for his simple statement. Now, our life is intricate and hot with clashing consciences. Thoreau is like cold, clear water against our fever.

His calm logic must have seemed madness to the fanatical New Englander. "How," he asks, "can we expect a harvest of thought who have not had a seed-time of character?" "Now that the republic—the *res publica*—has been settled, it is time to look after the *res privata*." "While England endeavors to cure the potato-rot, will not any endeavor to cure the brain-rot which prevails so much more widely and fatally?" "If a man does not keep step with his companions it is perhaps because he hears a different drummer." Such his questions: his life was his answer. Thoreau's father was a manufacturer of pencils. Thoreau perfected a better pencil than any known to that day even in London. His friends congratulated him upon his approach to fortune. He announced that he was done with pencils, now that he had made a good one. He lived in absolute economic freedom near Walden Pond. He proved that a margin of living could be won from even the severest struggle for existence. He sanctified that margin by writing a great book.

But his adventure was not an adventure of Escape. He temporarily retired, not to run away from men, but to establish Man—who, he considered, must come first. More clearly than Walt Whitman, he recognized the herd-quality of the American world (since he was also immune from its tragic beauty). He felt the need of measuring the conscious and creative strength of man against the accumulative weakness of the unconscious many. He expressed in his great book the want that is still with us: the establishment of an individual norm, the bringing-up of individuals.

And so, partaking of his experience, his prose is indestructibly solid beside the rhapsodies and fancies of the Transcendental School: cadenced and full like the pulse of his own life: America's first great prose.

Since he disbelieved in Slavery and was against the Mexican War, he declined to support a Government that went counter to his convictions. He refused to pay taxes and went to jail, and laughed. He was too healthy to be a martyr. He was too alive, as he put it, "to live under a government" many moments of his life. He, almost alone among the cultured citizens of New England, prized the spiritual riches of the Indians.

He went to Maine and Canada and spent long months with them, and had friends among them. Whenever the spirit moved him, he left his fields and went to Boston, and against the solemn warnings even of his friends, spoke out his convictions on public matters. And his words—not those of Washington and Jefferson—are the first words in the true Book of Liberty which America shall some day write. Such essays as *Civil Disobedience* and *Life Without Principle* are texts to-day for social and spiritual revolution. Their words are clear and weighty with the life that they expressed. So, also, such a masterpiece as *Walden*. It is the first conscious "Yea" of the Puritan world. As if he were dealing with the harried, iron-bound America of the Twentieth Century, Thoreau detects the deep hostility between the American's faith of "business' and life: he uncovers the false passions of possessiveness: he ridicules the fanatical direction of the Puritan Will which flings off life for a power it shall have no life to experience or to direct.

Thoreau had the prophetic quality. He saw whither the Puritan was tending. Part by part he studied the false doctrine of the prevailing American life, observed its inevitable fruits, weighed them and found them wanting. With a stern incision, he struck the call of his own life and values, and by the humble annals of his career gave them the proof of form.

It is true no less that this protest and this power of New England remained submerged. The inertia of degeneration brooded unbroken over the New England farms after Thoreau was gone and turned, by the grace of the pioneering god, into a naturalist.

The "Nays" still had it. New England became a manufacturing center, among other things, for lies: here were turned out the whole set of myths required by a Democracy in which five per cent. of the people owned sixty-five per cent. of the world they lived in: and controlled all of the political, cultural and economic channels. Reality was still for the most part an unavoidable terrain to be traversed before the next post-of-trade was reached. The intrinsic qualities of life were hurdles.

One finds, however, such comforting presences as that of Albert Pinkham Ryder.* While Whistler dazzled Europe with his exquisite designs, this man with a passion for the truth had come to being in Massachusetts. Ryder never burst altogether the shackles of his environs. He was too near the transcendentalists in intellectual interest. A part of him had a way of flying off from an opaque world into translucent æther. But another part of him—his eyes—was enamored of the sea, studied the matter of the clouds, grasped the secret of New England landscapes.

Such a picture as "The Race Track" is typical of his genius. A countryside, marvelously true in its dimensioned flow—and racing along the road an eerie rider, Death. Another of his works, he calls "Jonah and the Whale." A sea, overwhelmingly massive, mysteriously true in its turbulent heave: a struggling mite of a man in desperate prayer: and from the skies, the

* Born in New Bedford, Massachusetts, in 1847. Died in 1917.

vast visage of Jehovah dimly emergent. One feels that the shadowy rider in the former painting conveys the artist's vague acceptance of the reality of man; Jehovah in the latter his weak experience of God in a dense, hostile world. But since he paints such landscapes and such seas one forgives the transcendental remnant.

Ryder is the great American painter. He has brought to his vision of nature a remarkable energy and a remarkable science. The world to him is massive and dense and real. Also, it is suppressed, restricted, writhing with denial. It is *his* world—New England. A tortured reality, that still somehow has achieved the capacity to look upon itself.

Ryder, in his way, was also a queer man. He lived alone, imprisoned with his will. And his will was to recapture the reality of life. But that reality his Puritan forebears and his surroundings had hidden deep away. His struggle to recapture it was endless and full of travail. He worked years upon a little canvas: he worked like one possessed: like a mad lover he hunted his desire. And in the few paintings that his long years left us we understand what a passionate search it was. The pigment is thick with resolution. The frame is narrow, as if to shut in his world where his will could hold it. And the world lies there, unshakable, inexorable also. A world made hard and stern, but made dynamic and more real than ever by the Puritan denial. A world much of whose massivity and beauty comes from the heroic effort of the artist to achieve it. Tortured and shrunken, this world of Ryder: but vital since into it has gone the passion of the New Englander to re-attain what his birth has taken from him.

Not alone the denial of life makes up the Puritan cosmos: as well the protest against denial. The building-up, pitted against the tearing-down. This ambivalence of a tortured world speaks in Ryder. It speaks to-day even more clearly in the art of Robert Frost.

The poetry of Frost is of that excellent sort which it is hard to catalogue. It is lyrical. It is dramatic, since his books are—as he says—"of people." It is philosophic, since the tales he tells trace conscious lines about the boundaries of life. Fully, it is poetry—and of New England.

Nine generations of New Hampshire Frosts went to make this poet. And lest the congenital expression should fail in any count of the New England type, fate sent Frost's parents pioneering: the poet was born at the trail's end, in San Francisco. At ten, he was back where he belonged: in Massachusetts. At twenty-one, he was a farmer in New Hampshire. The arid soil brought forth better verse than crops. But the market for the crops was easier. For twenty years, Frost shipped his poems to the magazines and got his poems back. At last, in 1913, he sold his farm and took his family and his work to England. England supplied what America had evidently lacked: a publisher. In 1913, *A Boy's Will* appeared. In 1914, *North of Bos-*

ton made Frost a celebrity in London.* An American publisher then "discovered" the American poet. And when the War drove Frost back home, he was famous.

The painter of Nature is a painter of himself. Such a one was Ryder: such a one, for the most part, was Thoreau. Wistful individuals, these men, whose farthest discovery led alone to their own solitary souls. With Frost, however, the New England consciousness becomes objective: its world reaches the stage of differentiation. The beauty of Frost is populous.

Probably few even of the admirers of *North of Boston* and *Mountain Interval* are aware with what sort of men and women these lands are peopled. Let us see: Hired men dying without home or pride; sick women who have buried the one child and cannot swing their love beyond the grave that stares from the farm-window; black cottages from which life has at last rotted and glowed out; listless, inbred cousins, tallying an-

---

* It is interesting to note how England continues to give first honors to American expressions. Whitman, during most of his life, had his chief intellectual support in England. When the English novelist, Arnold Bennett, landed in America—I think in 1912—he made inquiries about "that great novelist of yours, Mr. Theodore Dreiser." Thereupon, the American press looked him up, and Dreiser was introduced to his own people. It was an Englishman, Mr. John Cowper Powys, who, lecturing in the United States and writing in the *New York Times,* gave the first popular impetus to Masters' *Spoon River Anthology.* Anderson's books were first accepted for publication by a London House. And Robert Frost was known in England before he was printed in America. . . . There is really no mystery in all this. England has no repressive and pervasive academies to make her deaf to American voices. In America, a large part of the *élite,* as we have seen, still holds that our literature is English. Well, most of it— the weak of it—still is. When the unregenerate American utterance is heard, this potent group resists it as a sure attack upon the dominion of the Puritan and Colonial point of view.

cestors for want of a more vivid present; women grown
old over dirty dishes, facing the madness that killed
their mothers; insane giant farmers caged like beasts
in a barn; lovers in fear of the dark for terror of their
own Nay-saying blood; maimed workers in saw-mills,
bought off with a pittance by shrewd lawyers from the
City; hill-wives that see no tree without the sweet
dream of hanging on it, and who disappear forever in
the forest, maddened and brutalized by silence; and the
home-stretch at last of the adventurers in life—a pile
of battered furniture, a rote of nodding habits, a bar-
ren farm. . . .

These quite literally are the people of his books—
the citizenry of Frost's New England. And yet, the
naming of them so is falsehood. For these are the materials of the poet: and Frost is a poet because he
creates them in the image of his own consciousness. He
does not distort them. He does not moralize about
them. He seems to put them nakedly enough and
brusquely upon paper. But he does manage somehow
in the process to make their misery live, their sterility
bear fruit, their sullen silence sing. And understanding Frost, detecting no foreign element within his
works, no imposition of will or wish or theory from the
outside upon them, one comes to see that the song and
the life and the beauty are also of New England—are
more true after all than the gross material from which
they issue.

One reads these amazing stories, with their fluent and
yet solid five-foot meters, and one learns from them
that New England is not dead, since Frost is so very

living. A starved, sick world perhaps. Rocky and stubborn and full of weeds. A world in which old passions lie stiff upon the ground and rot, and poison the water and blot the air. And yet, there is a fertile quality in this world. Even the rotting stirs. One comes to sense a rythm, indefeasible the more since it is so slow and hard. One comes to feel that after the long repose of bitterness and failure, lying upon New England, a new Beauty is being born.

Else whence the beauty of these poems? If ever beauty was the essential, inherent quality of life, it is in these colloquial tales. They have no trick of telling or of meter. The inadvertent reader could pocket one of them—figuratively—like a lump of uranium: and find soon enough how the latent radium burned him to the bone. So inherent, so mysterious-glowing is the poetry of Frost; must, therefore, be the element and the life that makes them—Puritan New England.

And yet, far removed as is this work from Masters'—who lies wounded upon the Battleground between the Past and the Present—it is almost equidistant from the work of Anderson and Sandburg. The fire of Frost remains within the bounds of its material. It lacks the excess energy of flame: perhaps the material is so dense and sodden that it absorbs it all. His poems are fiercely vital, but like New England their vitality is repressed: it has not burst into dynamic life. No aspiration, little faith rise from the world of Robert Frost. At most, a sardonic humor of resignation. This world is alive indeed, but it is not alive to the pitch of articulate desire, to the pitch where life becomes religious. Sandburg and Anderson are both more lyrical. Singing of Chicago, they are aware of their new gods. They are more conscious prophets. Frost is the more perfect artist.

I feel this synchrony in the New England poet and his land. Frost is intellectually conscious: but the source of his art is a direct intuitive reaction to the life about him. Even in his mental consciousness and discipline, this is so—for New England is an educated world. So, Frost depicts a land that is still precultural, a land glowing in the deliquescence of the old culture that has killed it, but not yet risen up to the new culture that shall once more give it life.

.   .   .   .

Frost is not alone. At the other extreme of his old, renewing world, is a sister-poet. Frost is the farmer, speaking from the backwoods north of Boston. Amy Lowell presides from her Academic Faubourg Saint Germain: Harvard and Brookline.   ,

The Lowells are one of those families so prodigal of power which explain New England perhaps more dramatically than any of its achievements. Since the early Eighteenth Century, Lowells have been jurists, agriculturalists, liberal leaders in Massachusetts. Then came James Russell Lowell—poet and essayist and diplomat, greatest of our intellectual snobs until Henry James succeeded to the title. The Lowell eminence thereafter shifted to a collateral branch. A brother of our poet is Abbott Lawrence Lowell, President of Harvard University: another brother is Percival Lowell, famed as an astronomer. And Miss Lowell herself supplies the radical balance to her more conforming family.

In Amy Lowell, the American cultural tradition at last strikes free from its ancient bondage whose arsenals-in-chief have been the Eastern universities: at last comes up to the American present. Miss Lowell was equipped to continue the mastery of her Puritan clan over the American world. Quite literally, she has trained her guns against her brothers. The elements of her upbringing, of her intellectual majority are the same as those which have kept the Colonial American, the unconscious Anglophile, on top. They speak in the United States Senate through such men as Henry Cabot Lodge; they preach in the schools through W. C. Brownell, Barrett Wendell, William Lyon Phelps; they set the journalistic standards in the leadership of the *Atlantic Monthly,* the *Boston Transcript,* the *New York Evening Post.* They are elements of very real mastery. In Miss Lowell they are at last devoted to the cause of American Expression, rather than American possession.

The reaction against English domination in American cultural life is not an attack on England. It is a plea for America. The young American has little in common, psychologically, with Great Britain. The Colonial classes are the exploiting classes. English culture is an apt means to the suppression of a nascent, non-Anglo-Saxon culture of our own. Community of language has made it simple by the stressing of English books to stifle our callow consciousness. And as America veered from the old English-colonial orbit to the

163

ethnic chaos from which a new world must be gathered, English culture has been a growing incubus upon us.

Now, one way to loose the hold of English literature is to stress the literatures of other European countries. Another is to stress our own. Miss Lowell does both. She has been a pioneer in popularizing modern French poetry among American intellectuals. She has done this, not by attitudinizing in London like Ezra Pound, but by really mastering the French spirit and, in book and lecture, transvaluing it into terms that American writers could make their own.

The last six years have marked the flower of a great American poetic renaissance. A score of earnest poets, many of them brooding for years in inarticulation, suddenly burst into song. Such spilth of force needed directing, such an array of naked and clashing colors needed composing. Miss Lowell has done a share which has been felt throughout America. She fought for hearers for the poets: she fought for tact and consciousness among the poets. She introduced methods of publicity and emphasis into the field of poetic education which had theretofore been consigned alone to the tasks of business and war. And yet, she did not lower her standards. She added the dignity of her position to the vitality of her time. She became an effective agent in the establishment of an American art.

Meantime, she wrote poetry of her own: and poetry which since its first appearance in 1912 has regularly improved. Miss Lowell is a pathfinder in English metrics. Her indebtedness to the *vers libre* of France and the forms of Japan she has been the first to acknowledge. They have served merely to midwife her own expression. Her range is wide. But she is possibly at her best in a sort of polyphonic narrative which also she variates with remarkable success. From poignant, subjective drama like *Patterns* to historical and social epic like *Guns and Keys: and the Great Gate Swings* her psychological touch is sure and her form rises to the dimensional pitch. Hers is probably the first serious attempt to link the historic pasts of our several American races to our own potential and emotional present. A real cultural background, a quick sensory experience and a firm conscious grasp of both must go into such work. Miss Lowell is unique among our artists in this consummation.

We have had academic poets whose academy was dead, whose poetry was dead. We have had emancipated poets who won their fragile freedom only at the price of blotting out the whole source of the past. In Miss Lowell, a literary tradition bridges once more into life: New England, the fountain-head of a past culture, again comes forward to nurture fledgling spirit.

The poise of Miss Lowell's work is the poise of strength. She is the first poet of our struggling age with a rounded culture like the European masters, and with the aptitude like them to reach into the past, embrace the present turmoil of affairs, and yet not lose her grip upon her art. The first true "man of letters" of Our America turns out to be a woman. . . .

. . . .

In 1905, a very quiet gentleman, having lived for

nearly seventy years in a very noisy world, wrote a book about his life. He was a gentleman inordinately modest and retiring—and yet a Puritan. So he called his "life" not a "life" but an "education." And the volume was issued privately to the extent of a hundred copies. Only his release in death has now released his book from the oblivion to which he had hopefully consigned it.

This gentleman was of the very soil of New England. His name was Henry Adams. His great-grandfather was John Adams, second President of the United States: his grandfather was John Quincy Adams, sixth President of the United States: his father was Charles Francis Adams, perhaps the best statesman of the three, Minister to England during the crucial years of the Civil War, and not Chief Magistrate of the Republic like them who had gone before, only because the political hegemony had swung by 1868 to the Middle-west and to a different sort of man. This Henry Adams was—for an Adams—obscure. His brother, the first president of a great transcontinental Railroad, was far better known. Henry was a scholar. He edited the *North American Review*, he wrote a half dozen standard works on American political affairs, he taught Mediæval History at Harvard. Then, at the end of his unobtrusive years, he put *The Education of Henry Adams* into form. With the result that his vision and his words will probably live on after his illustrious political sires are nothing but names.

This book is a very remarkable book indeed. If my reader had the time for but a single work in which to glean the significance and tragedy and promise of New England, I should send him to Henry Adams. "The Education" is the story of a civilization, the apotheosis of its destruction, the herald of its successor. It is a graceful touch of fate that this monument should have been made by an Adams—by a member of a family which perhaps as much as any brought that civilization to its height. "The Education" is, however, more than story: it is drama. But like a tragedy of Sophocles or Ibsen, its dynamic is altogether downward. The catastrophe is set. It is a play of the falling sun.

I cannot here aspire to give even the briefest picture of the vast canvas painted by modest Henry Adams. "The Education" is one of those vital books about which books will yet be written. What merely I may dwell on here is the direction of the education of this New Englander. For Adams is archetypical. And a whole starved and miserable race of brilliant men moves with his words.

Adams begins by stating how the fact of his birth was the promise of his failure. "Had he been born in Jerusalem under the shadow of the Temple," he says, speaking as he does throughout in the third person, "and circumcised in the Synagogue by his uncle the high priest, under the name of Israel Cohen, he would scarcely have been more branded, and not much more heavily handicapped in the races of the coming century, in running for such stakes as the century was to offer." What Adams means, wreathing out from his own personal and accentuated case, is that the America which New England was still in a sense to go on

167

ruling, was in reality swinging into an orbit where New England could not follow. The story of his life is the drama of his effort to catch up with the reality that forevermore eludes him, and with the truth that he cannot see. He goes through the cycle of New England culture. Under Eighteenth Century rationalism he was born. For the Puritan political régime of 1840 was nothing but its adaptation. Behavior and morals, as well as culture, in New England, were political. Its bible was the Constitution which it interpreted liberally according to economic moods quite as the minister interprets the sacred texts. Upon this political culture was overlaid the liberal culture of England and the Classical world. Adams finds these do not apply to the world he feels veering beneath his feet. And then, he discovers modern science and that world disappears.

Religiously, he follows the trail of modern science, from Darwin to Poincaré. And then, looking at his hands, he finds that there is nothing in them. The Puritan turns from the Dynamo which he discovers to have been a fraud, back to the Mediæval Virgin whom he wistfully envies since *she*, unlike the Dynamo, generated power. A whole century of discovery, of dynamic speculation, of frenzied fidelity to fact, brings him up at length to a barred Threshold—the threshold which he cannot pass, but to which, in his vicarious experience, he has brought New England and America also. That threshold opens to a new religion. In his later chapters, this rationalist, this skeptic, this student of political and physical science, speaks with the accents of Blaise Pascal. Science has been a messenger leading to the compulsion of a mystical conviction, effacing itself before the Goal it leads to. One does not sense in Adams what this new Gate discloses, upon which his whole life has been a laborious advance. One knows he calls his life a failure simply because of this. His years are the tragedy of his thwarted effort to escape from the Negation of his birth. The Virgin is dead. But, Adams points out, less dead somehow than Science which has killed her. His eyes look for Art, and all is flat around the old Cathedrals. Science has leveled knowledge to an exacter cognizance that knowledge does not exist. It has wiped out the myths of causation and effect, put a clear light on the impenetrable dark of Chaos: and added the compulsion of its own deliberate discourse to the human need of mystical experience.

All of this book is thus a cry for the new gods that Adams cannot see, for poring so close to the circumscribed facts of that empirical domain which Science—after claiming it would chain the universe—has itself reduced to an absurdity and a pin-point. "*Adams could only blunder back alone, helplessly, wearily, his eyes rather dim with tears, to the vague trail across the darkening prairie of education, without a motive, big or small, except curiosity to reach, before he too should drop, some point that would give him a far look ahead.*"

The last word of the Pioneer: the last sublimation of the Puritan will-to-power and to knowledge upon the plane of empiric fact. Adams did not find that point he sought upon his darkening prairie. That point was above his prairie and he could not leave his prairie.

He died first. But he died—child of political empiry, of rational discipline, of scientific dedication—he died wistfully worshiping the mystery of Force, adoring the blind fecundity of woman: with faint hands groping after Life which of all things the Puritan had no doctrine and no technique to embrace.

But New England had said "Yea" to Life. Now at last, Life might come into New England. . . .

VII. NEW YORK

A keen lady from Paris confessed to me: "I love your city of New York. But its inhabitants—that is different!" She did not understand. Here was a distinction forced upon her senses, beyond her European scope. In Europe, city and inhabitants were one. She could not understand the justice of her own remark.

And yet, she had touched on a deep thing. New York is a resplendent city. Its high white towers are arrows of will: its streets are the plowings of passionate desire. A lofty, arrogant, lustful city, beaten through by an iron rhythm. But the men and women who have made this city and whose place it is, are lowly, are driven, are drab. Their feet shuffle, their voices are shrill, their eyes do not shine. They are different indeed from their superb creation. Life that should electrify their bodies, quicken them with high movement and high desire is gone from them. And if you seek that life, look to the flashing steel and stone that stands above them, look to the fierce beat of their material affairs. America is the extraverted land. New York, its climax. Here, the outside world has taken to itself a soul—a towering, childish soul: and the millions of human sources are sucked void.

The base of the New York world is a weary people.

The margin of energy whence spring the higher impulses of men is sapped away. A people turned debtor to its own affairs. A bankrupt people, unable with the repose of night to meet the fearful drainage of the day. The city is too high-pitched, its throb too shattering-fast. Nervous and spiritual fiber tears in such a strain. The average New Yorker is caught in a Machine. He whirls along, he is dizzy, he is helpless. If he resists, the Machine will mangle him. If he does not resist, it will daze him first with its glittering reiteration, so that when the mangling comes he is past knowing. He says he is too busy, and wonders why. He means, that all preference of act is gone from him. He must face to-day without that inner light which can alone illumine it: he must face to-morrow without that seed of dream, by which alone it might be rendered fecund.

Observe the New Yorker. . . . The downtown hour of luncheon. The taking of food is naturally a restful sacrament. Even the undegraded brute is meditative when he eats. But the New Yorkers stream from their offices and shops and lofts, and crowd into food-pens, gorge and rush away. The millionaire in his luncheon-club atop some skyscraper eats in a nervous bustle like the shop-girl and the clerk at their cluttered counters. A quiet man with spiritual occupations to preserve his nerves and sharpen them could not thrive in the din where Business takes food. Nor does he. His nerves are dulled, his receptivity to the less gross qualities of life go from him. But, at least, he is able to lunch without a sense of outrage.

The day's work is done. The houses spew out their human provender, having absorbed what energy they held. The streets rise with the poured human waste, they become choked sluices leading to the subways. In the fetid stations, men and women stand packed as no Western rancher packs his cattle. Masses of them, mute, unangry, wait for the next train to glide in beside them and slough off its loadful. The doors slide open, the brackish human flow pours through, the doors cut like knives the mass within from the discarded mass without. The train crawls with its inert freight.

As the thick coagulation moves towards the trains, it buys evening papers. These are designed to catch the dulled attention of the molecular units, men and women and girls. Huge headlines, rancid tales of lust and plunder, crude cartoons shriek into the face of the New Yorker; the lash of their sensational lies flick him to a semblance of attention. No less would touch him.

In the evenings, he and his wife or he and his "girl" go to the "movies." The children also. And here again, the low consciousness to which his city has reduced him is carefully sustained. The American frontier produced new modes of amusement. The pioneer was brutalized with physical exhaustion, and yet too nervously high-keyed by his hard work to move direct from it to so far an opposite as sleep. For him, the dance-hall, raw whiskey, the thrill of gambling for life-stakes, and shooting. In New York, the weariness of the pioneer has stiffened into an unchallenged norm. But the prudence of the Puritan, if nothing else, has robbed him of his revolver and his faro. He seeks their simulacra on the screen.

But this New Yorker is no true pioneer. The impulse of acquisition quickened the race that passed before. That race came first. Then came the city that was its product. And now another race that is the product of the city. The pioneer was vital and fluent. A living impulse made him. The New Yorker of today is stiff and slack: he has been fathered by steel and broken by it. So also is this difference mirrored in his amusements. His dramas of the screen are dull. The characters move like automata: wooden, devitalized.

In the warm weather, the fetor of the "movies" bears in on the New Yorker and makes him seek the amusement of the sea-shores. The first thing to be observed about the beaches where he goes to be amused, is that he has done his best to hide away the sea. It takes energy to look upon the sea: it takes just that capacity for meditation and repose which the man without energic margin lacks. The New Yorker has no power with which to meet the speaking solitudes of Nature. If it is very hot, he may go into the ocean for a bath. Then, he turns his back. He seeks the scenic railroads, the jazz-bands, the ticklers, the shoot-the-chutes, the myriad mechanical contraptions which bump and pound and twist and jostle him in such resorts as Coney Island.

When Maxim Gorki was in America he said that our amusement-parks were the most mournful places he had ever seen. For this, he was called names by our properly indignant American authorities—the same who snubbed him and made his visit a humiliation because of a technical lack in his marriage license. Yet, unfortunately, Gorki was right. No person in whom joy is overflowing will resort to a machine that stands him on his head and spins him on his ear, to shake it out. These are makeshifts of despair. America is a joyless land. And nowhere is this so crying-clear as in the places of New York—Broadway, the "movies," Coney Island—where Joy is sought.

The hard dazzle of Broadway by night is the very antithesis of gayety. It is business. Broadway's brightness is the sum of advertisements flashing petticoats and constipation-cures against the blackened heavens. Two living things are shrunken and obscured in the "Great White Way": the sky and the men and women. Joy is the daughter of Strength: the birth of a vitality that has no way but overflowing. Pioneer and Puritan and Industrialist have made New York. And like the sky, Joy has been shadowed out. Its citizens are worn too weak: their stomachs have too long been empty: they must beware even of strong illusions. Melodrama shrinks to an emasculated form: farce is anæmic: comedy is unknown. Men who have no time for play grow wild over the fabricated rivalry of professional baseball teams which they have never seen: women who have no time to love seek the stir of a remembered longing in some canned romance.

.   .   .   .

This is the Lump that lies beneath the bright towers of New York. Two leavens are at work upon it.

The first of these is of the first importance. The Stream has gone westering now for near two hundred years. Innumerable flows of it. It came to rest in the pockets of the Western mountains. It eddied out among the middle plains. Or it pushed over both, only to be stopped at the Pacific. In these seeming resting-places, often it was restless. For it was still Desire. Much of it settled. Much of it flung back over the channels it had made in going. From the fruit ranches of California back to San Francisco. From the prairies back to Chicago. From the hills of Missouri and Kentucky back to Richmond and Saint Louis. From all America back to New York.

This throw-back upon the city from the West, the South, the North brings to New York its restless inquiry, its insatiate search. A true leaven. For these men and women—boys and girls, since such they are in the main—are the most self-conscious of their groups. They have left the home-town and the home-farm because they were dissatisfied. And they are hungry, because they have tasted the food of their native life and found it wanting. For the most part, they are the intellectually roused. And since intellect is the mere spear-head of the human being, it is safe to say they are the vital. What they have found wanting is precisely the pioneer existence, the Puritan culture which their Fathers have set up. Often, their fathers are strong, stern men: last living remnants of the old frontier. And these restless ones possess that energy, and turn it in revolt against the fixed decisions of their fathers—the same energy which pushed *them* west-

ward. Their hands, once more, are empty. Quite like
their fathers, they go forth to hunt—though in an opposite direction.

They pour into New York from a thousand towns
and colleges. They are the seekers of a world nearer
their heart. Inevitably, they are the artists and the
writers. For such are men and women who desire to
create a world of their own to live in. They congre-
gate and there rises up a buzz of voices from among
them. The vast horizontal Stream that fertilized a
continent strains now to become vertical, in order to
fertilize a heaven.

And here—to meet them, to reinforce them—a new
leaven works upon the city. Europe. . . .

Up to thirty years ago, there was little of Europe
in our consciousness. Millions of immigrants came
in. Europeans before they left Europe. But pioneers
when they reached New York. The swing of America
within the European orbit came when pioneering had
already subdued America, made of it a home. It de-
pended less on men than on finance: less on men than
on ideas. The Cable was developed. The great Capitals spoke more casually with New York. American
industry flowed over the seas, and the conduits of Exchange were opened. Along them, Thought came back.
Publishers grew fat and needed European books.
Ladies grew rich and begged for European music.
The great steamers brought visitors that were not
pioneers, and carried the pioneers of an earlier day on
cultural pilgrimages back to Europe.

The rebels from the West met Europe in New York

and made it theirs. They took Europe to their studio-altars in Greenwich Village * and fell on their knees before it. One great Hate they had brought, in their retracing steps—one Hate from Vermont and from Ohio and from Arizona: the Hate of Puritan ideals. And here were the minds of Europe coming to teach them how to love! Logical voices of France, mystical pleadings of Russia, protests of the Celt—Moore and Shaw—against the Puritan at home. What a godsend for the hungering New Yorker! What a leaven!

Slowly, the ferments moved through the lump of the Eastern seaboard. Slowly, New York became the nervous city. For Europe, invading America, could not hope to conquer. The American stuff was too firm and too immense, too willfully set for that. Europe was alien and remote as never before. All it could hope to bring—from Ibsen to Dostoievski—was conflict. And conflict unresolved—emotional conflict—means *neurosis*.

It would, of course, be more accurate to say that Europe helped materialize the conflict. The impulse throwing back the Stream upon the eastern city was in reality a complex of all those yearnings and desires which a world of pioneers had not admitted. A sleeping beauty. For its awakening, the youth went hungry to New York. And now, groping in the Amer-

*In a way the *Quartier Latin* of New York, since here the young writers and artists gather together. In a way not, since the University life is in another part of town. So called after the old village which was once there and which New York long since swallowed.

ican dark, he saw a light from Europe! Europe had
been there before. But no ready—no restless America to face it. America had been too absorbed in her
fierce preoccupation. If Europe came, Europe was
swept in. Now, however, this same energy was once
more searching. What it needed was the vision of another way, the munition of fresh ideas, to help it battle at home for its own direction.

For each self-conscious American, however, who deliberately drew the inspiration of Europe to our shore,
there were a thousand others who had no such power,
but who, now Europe had come, did grow aware of it.
These unnumbered ones had also their sleeping
beauty: that part of them which yearned and was
barred by the iron outer world. Industrialism holds
the seed of its own dissolution because it can satisfy
but a tithe of the humans whose suffrage it requires.
Each American had been a pioneer: had had the hope
of wealth. But not each American can become a capitalist. True, Labor in this country is cheated of its
own resurgence by the common myth that any work-
man may reach the employer's class. But in a nation
of vastly concentrated wealth, that Myth must go,
however hardy myths may be among us. Many sons of
prosperous men are realizing that it was the lax opportunity of an open country which made their fathers
rich, and that this opportunity is gone. Technical
specialists are learning that for the most part they are
serfs to wealth. Writers and lawyers and teachers
grow aware of their true estate. Farmers observe
the growth of tenancy among them. The Myth is still

strong. The suppressed thirsting after life is still submerged enough to make the American people among the least articulate and the least artistic. But the thirst has long been there, however mutely. And now, in the widespread disappointment, it made widening numbers stir to the new incentives—rebirth, revolt— of invading Europe.

The narrowed industrial world has no gates—even if it would—to open. But here are the mounting murmurs of many groups, rebellious and intent: and there are the voices of Europe, which echo infinitely farther than they are understood. The repression partially lifts. New York grows restless, nervous, sick: full of desires that are black since it can not give them light, and that are ghosts since it dare not let them live.

Therefore, a neurotic rather than a lumpish city. But whether the *Sturm und Drang* of youth or an organic weakness, who may say? And yet, the city that threw such light as Whitman against the darkness of a world is surely not altogether feeble.

In the nervous tension of New York, the mutterings of American unrest have risen to a shriek. But also, they have become the voice of Order. New York lies between invading Europe and America. A frontier city. And a self-conscious one. Here, if anywhere, you must look for the leader and the critic.

.　　.　　.　　.　　.　　.　　.

There is one place and one man in whom the creative meanings of these words meet, as not elsewhere, in the city. The man is Alfred Stieglitz. Possibly, the place is Alfred Stieglitz also. We shall see. . . .

Stieglitz was born as near New York as most New Yorkers seem ever to be born: across the Hudson River, in New Jersey in 1864. By 1900, he was world-famed as a photographer. America is the land of the Machine. In no other nation is the mechanical fact so close a part of life and growth. Other nations found the Machine in their maturity. To America, it was the toy and the tool of childhood. Perhaps therefore it is not accident, that the powerful vision which is Stieglitz should first have found itself through a machine.

The photography of Stieglitz is an intensely individual possession. In his views of New York—of riverfront, factory and trainyard—he masters the dominant details of industrial life, and makes them serve the unifying vision of human spirit. At a time when Europe was still groping toward it, Stieglitz had found the true *abstract* of art:—not in the avoidance of representation nor in the ignoring of detail, but in their mastery and fusion to an essential vision. His best work demonstrates this. His portraiture and studies of the nude have won a field for the camera which I, for one, would have considered forever beyond its scope. He has achieved plasticity and intense subjective interpretation of the human form. He has mastered a deep reality and lifted it up to his own terms. He is perhaps to-day the one major American in art.

By 1905, Stieglitz had become a unique figure in American photography. His *Quarterly*, "Camera Work" was already two years old. He was the leader of such leaders as Steichen, Coburn, Käsebier and

White. Photography, however, having been made respectable, now threatened to be modish. The blighting hand of the patron millionaire was laid upon it. The true craftsmen were menaced with the alternative of joining the commercial crowds or disappearing. Stieglitz and Steichen found a couple of rooms at No. 291 Fifth Avenue, and announced the *Photo-Secession*. The place was in the heart of affluent New York. Soon, it had far transcended its photographic purpose. It became simply "291."

It is hard to speak clearly of "291"—although it can of course be done:—of what it was and meant. It has no precedent that I know of in any other city. Its influence has been too subtly wide for any sure perspective in 1919.

Fifteen years ago, when "291" was born, New York was far more a noisy desert than it is to-day. The generation which is now at last making itself heard was mute: even the middle-generation was still dumb in travail. Stieglitz brought to his modest little rooms America's first views of modern European art. Even for us, it is hard to realize what this meant in 1905. Here Cézanne was introduced: Rodin was shown—his water-colors even before Paris knew them. Here, Matisse, Picasso, Rousseau and the others invaded an incredibly hostile world. A true invasion by Europe. The newspapers jeered and raged. Stieglitz was accused of indecent conduct. New York, sauntering the Avenue on idle afternoons, came and laughed aloud. Stieglitz had the deafness of one who hears a sweeter music.

And then the inevitable happened. Scattered in New York, lost in the nerveless welter of a continent, were single men and women: hungry, at times even for bread: all of them spiritually homeless. "291" drew them and banded them together. Others whose hunger had driven them to Europe, came back starving the more since they had feasted. America seemed a bitter desert to these men. The weak and comfortable could not stand it. They returned to London, to Paris, to Munich and Berlin. Only an heroic will could make the hardier, the more passionate for service, brave America's inclement weather. These, "291" saved from disaster. The present brilliant generation is unthinkable without this home and this man, Stieglitz. He was not rich, although the gossip of New York early decided that such madness as his must have a purse behind it. But he found support, if necessary he found food, for his needy friends. If they had no place to sleep, "291" became a place to sleep in. He showed their pictures, he found courageous buyers (no one of whom but has won by his investment), he schooled the solitary critics who were willing to cease sputtering oaths. And at the end, artists like John Marin, Marsden Hartley, Max Weber, Arthur Dove, Henry Walkowitz, Maurice Sterne, Georgia O'Keeffe emerged, with strengthened wings—able to fly alone. In 1905, no art was more backward in America than painting. In less than ten years, no art was more progressive: no art had so intelligent and compact a public: no group of creative workers was so self-conscious, so hardy as the radical American painters.

And yet, saying this, I have not touched the main significance of Alfred Stieglitz. . . .

You stepped away from the brittle brilliance of Fifth Avenue. A tiny elevator carried you up a way, and you came upon a couple of gray rooms. "291." The door was always open. Perhaps, Stieglitz was not in. Possibly no one, although this was rare. Only some water-colors of Cézanne or the latest plastic harmonies of Marin. If you were a thief, you could have stolen. No thief did. It was the one open door in burglar-harried Manhattan. Except some churches. And this is the point. You were in a church consecrate to them who had lost old gods, and whose need was sore for new ones.

"291" is a religious fact: like all such, a miracle. It is an altar where talk was often loud, heads never bared, but where no lie and no compromise could live. A little altar at which life was worshiped above the noise of a dead city. Here was refuge, certain and solitary, from the tearing grip of industrial disorder. When you were heartsick with all the dominance of death, you came to "291" and you found life. No place could be so holy as this place, for no place could be less holy than the world around it. New York was a lying and destroying storm: "291" was a candle that did not go out, since it alone was the truth.

Most of the time when you were there, you found Stieglitz. Otherwise the remaining times could not have been so pregnant, since after all it was of him they were pregnant. . . . A short, lean man, dressed like a conservative broker. A shock of graying hair

whose tangles seemed to fling off tangents of rebellion.
A mustache that bristled. Ears hair-tufted like a
faun's. Hands forever working as if they were mold-
ing life. Eyes too pent with passion and with dream
to flash their vision lightly. A man so natural, it took
the art of unlearning artificial ways to understand him.

When he talked, you became aware of a strange
thing. He was in no hurry. He swept back perhaps
twenty years: phase over phase his words rolled on,
careful, clear, until his speech seemed a convoluted
form, measurable, solid, moving like three dimensions.
And with the silence, you looked and found that he
had given you no brittle point, no isolated intellectual
opinion: but an experience of life in which such points
and such opinions were trivial details. A conversation that was art: massively formed, instinct with the
passion and intuition of his life. A conversation that
was a discipline. No swift approximation. Stieglitz
seemed, by some miracle, to have time even to talk!

I have never heard him preach. He gave you—gave
any one that would—his life, formed into compelling
words. And his life was so brave and so august a
thing, that you were in no need of preaching. You
came to him with the voice in you that spoke for beauty
drowned by the booming Nay of the world. And in
your nervous state, you gripped your chair and forced
yourself to listen. A sudden stimulant that must have
dropped you limp at the end had better pleased you.
Better than the slow, solid voice of Stieglitz, wander-
ing over years, picking out the fearfully consequent
words that passed between himself and some one else

in 1893. But he held forth, till the long beat of his living meaning caught you, and polarized you, and at length lifted you up, recharged. So you went out, with that voice once more vibrant: vowing it should not be dismayed and that even some day it should be heard. A man quite unsentimental, unmoralistic, a firm lover, a ruthless and unhating fighter. The New Yorker of our day perhaps above all others who has not been caught by our day's delirium. For neither did he avoid it, nor succumb to it: neither hate it nor adore it. He saw it. Which means he saw beyond it. It became material to his vision, and to the vision of those he strengthened. During crucial years, this man was altogether given up to a cause that in New York seemed hopeless: the ridiculous cause of life for life's sake, the cause of self-expression. For many, of many sorts, he was the preserver of faith, the great life-giver. Until that cause was hopeless no longer. And for no weightier reason than himself. . . .

Alfred Stieglitz is a Jew. He takes up the ancient destiny where the degenerate Jew whom we have observed had let it fall. He is the prophet. And his ways are near to the old ways of his people. He has been the true Apostle of self-liberation in a destructive land. His means was art. But art always as a means. Stieglitz is primarily the Jewish mystic. Suffering is his daily bread: sacrifice is his creed: failure is his beloved. A true Jew. To him, art is simply the directest conduit to human consciousness—to self and to the world; the most urgent incentive left to man. For the more surely a man finds himself, and

186

finds the world he lives in, the more surely he finds God. Art with a message is a profanation. The artist must simply be the servant of the soul, worshiper of the revelations of his life. As such, Stieglitz made a place for him in the American world, gave him warmth and courage. He is a man who has seen God and who has dared to speak. . . .

Others in New York are marking this new rising of the Jew. Plenty of others. But as there is one Stieglitz, so there is one Leo Ornstein.

Ornstein was born in Russia in 1895. The broken Revolution of 1905 implicated his family. They escaped to the Manhattan slums. Ornstein became a remarkable pianist. He was touring in Europe just prior to the War: and there, the energy that surged through Debussy, Schoenberg, Skriabin, Stravinsky, Bloch, unconsciously released his own. He made stirring music.

Ornstein's music is not Russian. Since there is no good American music save that of the Indians and Negroes, his music is as American as any. He calls it Hebrew. And he is right. It is the full-throated cry of the young Jew in a young world. Background of the Old—passion of pain and storm and deep repression. But upon it, breaks of fire, interstices of light, America's release. The weight of the sorrow of the Jew like a loading atmosphere about him. And the Jew's intricate response: reasoning and wailing, the birth of faith, the tidal pour of energy in faith. New hope, new deed, new life. An answer to the lamentations of the Jewish fate in Ornstein's music: a sort of angry joy, lust of a new world's conquest. Hebrew the seed: American the fruit.

Walt Whitman would have loved the song of Leo Ornstein. He would have said: "This is my brother singing, who has been long cast down and who now starts with me upon the Open Road." A mere start it is. Whether Ornstein, himself, with his undoubted genius, will travel it far, no one may say. But when all our people have at last come through suffering to longing, and thence to the release in life, they will find in them music. And it will be American. It will be near kin to the music of Leo Ornstein, with his burden of a stifled race and his clashing pæans of release.

Close to Ornstein is a critic whom it is appropriate to mention here. First, however, a slight digression about another. . . .

The obsessive beat of American life, the dominant Puritan mind, made impossible before our generation any true acceptance of European art. Europe fascinated us. But we were emotionally too absorbed and involved, even to understand the reason for our fascination. At first, only England was real. And the insularity of England seemed to become more cramped as it traveled Westward. Then, American curiosity crossed the Channel. A small but significant class began to crave news of the artists of France and Germany and Russia. Doubtless this early craving was the herald of a still mute sense of relationship with Continental Europe: of the need of striking clearer of Great Britain. But in its callow form, it was the mere hunger for spice, the search of snobbery. American intellectuals wanted to read of Paris and Berlin, as the shopgirls, of Newport and Palm Beach. To supply this need, there arose a school of criticism which was in reality a school of gossip. Its master was James Gibbon Huneker.* Huneker is, in a way, a tragedy. He was bound by the middle-generation. He was too caught up by every lien of his emotional life in the isolating beat of the pioneering world. And he wanted to interpret Europe. His mind went to Europe: went honestly: but went without his heart. His heart, like Dreiser's, stayed with the childish frontiering mob: but unlike Dreiser's, did not swing his mind along. A divorce of energy in Huneker that has limited his work. He studded his pages with clever small talk of Paris and Munich and Berlin. He called Flaubert and Nerval and Hello and Strauss and Stirner and Satie by familiar names. He could know their mistresses, their tastes in drink. He could not know their meaning. But his American audiences knew less. And they were eager. Huneker, therefore, feeding them from the new tree of knowledge, fullfilled a function. He marked the early stirring of America beyond what might be called the nutritive problems of her childhood: her first efforts to widen her subjective world by visiting Europe. His hosts of imitators have simply turned his natural callowness into a trivial and ugly pose. But

---

* Huneker was born in Philadelphia in 1860. The title of a few of his books will suggest the sort of purveyance which they supplied: *Chopin, Melomaniacs, Franz Liszt, Iconoclasts—a Book of Dramatists, Egoists—a Book of Supermen, Promenades of an Impressionist, The Pathos of Distance.*

in the advent of such critics as Paul Rosenfeld * we understand that their day is over.

Rosenfeld was born in an hour when the pioneer grip was somewhat loosed. America, hungry at last for spiritual food, could honestly go abroad and get it. Rosenfeld could take his heart, together with his mind, to Europe, without danger of loss to his American nature. So he did. And now, as opposed to Huneker, his struggle is to bring back his conscious mind to his own land. Rosenfeld, it is true, has not matured to the conscious discovery of a native life for his interpretation. But at least, if he writes best about French and Russian music, he manages to distil from them an experience that is his own: an experience that is American. Skriabin or Debussy make a certain intimate register upon his mind. Faithfully he records it. And in so far as he is a young American, quick with the adventure of his generation, that register is valid.

Besides, that register is beautiful. He is far advanced indeed from the smart small-talk of the little Hunekers. He brings to his subject a fine æsthetic apparatus: a discipline of taste. He gives to the American reader a reaction that is rare, an understanding that is true. We have so many critics who write of Europe in order to feel themselves in the company of the great, that it is good to acknowledge Rosenfeld who writes of Europe in order to bring great strength to our own struggling consciousness of beauty. In his service of introduction to America of such composers as Ornstein and Ernest Bloch, Rosenfeld gives us high

* Born in New York in 1890.

hope of what he will achieve when at last he feels within him the spiritual strength to interpret our own expressions to our own understanding.

One more example—a poet—to typify the character of the Jew's renascence in his new free world.

New York has been too overwrought and too repressed to give us untrammeled artists like Robert Frost, sheer singers like Sandburg. James Oppenheim * comes to the song of life along more conscious and more mediate paths—the paths of politics and science.

Oppenheim has studied deep in the new psychology: he is tossed with the social fever of the world. He is the student singer. He draws within him new observances—jottings of analysis and human law. They weigh him down, oppress him. And then, in the swell of his personal reaction, they rise up again in song. Revolution of self in a new-won consciousness, revolution of the world, in a new-won hope: such are his subjects.

Oppenheim is the absorbing, pondering Jew. He is more flushed with the kaleidoscope of the outer world —more flung and veered with it than he himself suspects. He registers the American's subservience to the sheer bulk of desire which surrounds him in factory and machine. He mirrors not alone this primeval force, but also America's adoration of it. Often the form of his mirroring is crude and quick like the form of an American town. He is the laureate of our immediate, distraught world. The accents of *Songs for*

* Born in St. Paul, Minn., 1882.

the New Age, The Book of Self convey the problems
and the uplifted passions of the marketplace, the draw-
ing-room. It is also typical that he should be the
preacher—the exhorter, often to the detriment of the
poet. He is voluptuous in ideas, rather than in forms.
His lines have the downward gravity of thought, rather
than the soaring curves of dream. He is a true product of New York, the self-conscious city: singer of a
world in which social and intellectual doctrines clash,
and the clearer sweeter passions lie submerged.

.   .   .   .

Needless to say New York is the Capitol of our
critics.

Among them, representative of the middle-generation that gave us Masters and Dreiser, is Henry L.
Mencken. Mencken was born in Baltimore in 1880.
He opened his critical career by espousing the cause
of Nietzsche in a land full of Methodist churches. Before long, he loomed on the gray American horizon as
a sort of capering Saint George come to slay the Puritan Dragon. Mencken was well armed. He knew his
Dragon. He had a head full of instances, plenty of
red-blood and a prose mount that could charge like an
army or pirouette like a pony-ballet. He knew the
weaknesses of his elected monster. He attacked him
with ridicule, innuendo, the parry of superior erudi-
tion, the gusto of his own hearty, somewhat Rabelaisian
nature. He fought for his emerging generation. He
fought for the generation yet unweaned. To-day, the
authority of Mencken over the critical flatlands of the
United States is a thing beautiful and delicious to be-

hold. A whole horde of survivors from the first Puritan battles copy his adjectives, drink in his taste like the heady wine it is. And even the opposition—Old Masters like Brander Matthews—sidle up to the great Mencken and beg him to be kind.

Within his field, Mencken has done a yeoman's service. Unlike Huneker he has stayed at home. Like him, it is true, he is not wholly free of the old gods, he is caught in the same spiritual interregnum. But the zeal with which he leads the attack on Puritanism, Colonialism, the Academic, could inhere only in a man who was so near these enemies as to be touched by them. Mencken's hate is dynamic because it is subjectively purposeful: because it is defensive. Such must be the guidance of all hands that go out to strike.

And now, rising from the ground which the men of the middle-generation have done so much to fertilize and clear, the critics of young heart. A common defensive hate binds them together: they wage implicit, almost instinctive War on the pantheon of Puritan-Industrial ideals. But as they move in search of the creative values—values in taste, articulation, life— which shall save America, their ways diverge. I can do no more than suggest a few of the directions, by singling out a few of the men who take them. . . .

Philip Littell * is enamored of the seclusiveness of art. He comes by his love, of an old tradition. Bravely he seeks to carry it into the present. He ventures forth into the modern havoc and makes his Quiet there. Like Rosenfeld, he is sincerely at home in much

* Born in Brookline, Massachusetts, in 1868.

of European thought: and justifies his absorption by transforming it into American expression. Francis Hackett * keeps closer to his political friends. An Irishman by birth, he is a brilliant interpreter of Ireland's central Cause: and he brings his power of contentious discourse into a literary field too free of the zest of curious wit, too likely to be heavy when it is not flippant. Shaw, of course, fascinates Hackett. One regrets at times that his political vision should muddle him a bit when he discusses such novelists as Wells and Bennett. But one forgives him, since he is aware also of Anderson and Dreiser and Vachel Lindsay: since they move him to true service in the cause of American expression.

Most of our worthy critics write for the so-called "intellectual" magazines. If fame carries them beyond to the wide bourgeois world, they take their exclusive manner with them: let the bourgeois—who love to—gape. In one critic of rare distinction, we have a different fact. Clarence Day, Jr., belongs to our aristocracy of letters. He is keenly sensitive, finely poised, untrammeled. But he has the strange whim of wanting to talk with multitudes of people! I know of but one way that a critic of delicate temper and clear soul can talk with the American middle-masses: and that way is Day's. He talks in whimsical parables, in bright discursive instances, in fables full of wit. He chats. He garnishes his pages with comic drawings of his own. And behold, the unregenerate readers of a widely circulated magazine take in his

* Born in Kilkenny, Ireland, in 1883. Came to America in 1900.

eclectic wisdom, his reticent plea for what is courageous and high in the world's letters, and actually
enjoy it! Clarence Day out of his human wish to bring
the message of rare spirits to many minds is creating
a new critical form: a form that is a function of the
vague and vast American hunger for new gods, and
that functions well. His pages are a triumph. Possibly, they are a promise. Do they not point to the
Bridge which all true artists seek, between themselves
—expressers of a world—and the world that they express?

.   .   .   .

Rather an essayist than a critic is Van Wyck
Brooks.* It is he who almost singly seems to have set
himself the task of organizing an American tradition †
which shall, unlike the traditions of our schools, bring
birth to an articulated people. Brooks is the scholar
with creative vision. He thinks in dynamics. He looks
back over the arid stretches of our Past and seeks to
transvalue them, so that youth may grow sustenance in
the fields where professors—cultural sextons—now
merely guard their dead. A *usable past* he looks for.
In turning his own fertile vision back, he finds.

Brooks is a subtle, often elusive writer. So subtle
that America has not yet awakened to the great sweep

---

* Born in Plainfield, New Jersey, in 1886.

† A beginning was undoubtedly made in John Macy's *Spirit of
American Literature,* which appeared in 1913. At that time, most
of the newer voices which we have studied were not yet clearly
audible. Macy had no conscious present by which to gauge the
past. But in his attempt to focus our cultural background, syn-
thetize the impulses of our leaders, and trace a dynamic will pushing through them to us, he did the work of a literary pioneer.

of his imagination: so elusive that he has not yet quite
faced America with his message. Perhaps we need
first a little more of Mencken. The spirit of Stieglitz
is not alien to the critical work of Brooks. He studies, not to dissect, but to heal. He is lit with a passion, also, to create America. He works to help it
find its legs, to set it up and point it forward, and *make
it move*. The intellectual reading public is at a stage
where it likes gossip and individual instances: the small
change of the critic. Brooks has no time for such. He
is caught in a vast dream of giving America a brain
and a nervous system, *so it can go;* he does not stop
to discuss joints and fingers. He is our prime co-
ordinator. And perhaps for this very reason, he has
not yet come into his own among a people who are still
in the baby stage of playing with their toes.

The focus of the eye of Brooks will not relent nor
narrow down from the full American scene. But it is
not on that account unseeing. His motive is a devotion that makes him brother to the poet: but, as I have
said, his method is the scholar's. He has a concise intelligence through which to strain America. Intuition
bases and caps—as it must all knowledge—the careful structures of his studies. But they are not on that
account less real, nor less detailed than the work of
those purblind and more popular critics who, seeing
only the facts at their nose, see nothing.

Quite simply, Brooks is creating a consciousness of
American life. Such books as this one could not have
been written without his pioneering work. Whatever

consciousness we have had so far has been the result of vast and deliberate exclusions. A consciousness that would fit the citizen for pioneering, prepare him to exploit, or to remain the victim of exploitation. Roughly, a consciousness that denied life and feared life and debauched life into a miserable means to a dead end. Against this, the message of Walt Whitman could not prevail in its generation. A lyric torrent—one of the most massive in all literatures—the *Leaves of Grass* could not fertilize America until it was brought in contact *with* America. Upon such work Brooks is intent: to bring the American soul to its reality, among other things, to Whitman. For the new consciousness which he is helping to create is one in which all life shall enter, and which shall have no end save to bring all life to its fruition.

Van Wyck Brooks studies his problem through the data of direct expression—the data of literature and art. He has essentially a non-political mind. Now, it so happens that of the very few quick minds in America to-day, the great majority are politically turned. We are a nation of voters: a nation of commercial schemers. The one door which the Puritan culture did not shut was that of governmental thought. It is a door which most Americans who think at all are wont to take. The fact that Brooks could not take it explains at best the long fight he is having for attention. Fortunately, however, New York has given us another essayist—another creative critic—who has grasped America by the more accustomed handle.

Randolph Bourne is dead at the age of thirty-two.* But we who are his friends and love him are convinced that he will not altogether die from the American world. He was a hunchback. A great, seeking head upon a broken body. One forgot the cripple. One saw only the exquisite hands, hands like the music he loved best to play—and the deep gray eyes. One heard only the clear bravery of his talk and knew that the hands and the eyes were speaking.

Agony of war. Irony preserved him through the Night. And as the Dawn broke grayly, irony struck him down. The crippled body passed. So the hands and the eyes were silent.

He himself, dying, understood the irony best of us all. A cripple, poor, helpless against the cold of New York winters, helpless at the last against the ugly temper of the Herd, Bourne enjoyed life! He won miraculously from his struggle a margin of energy for laughter and for wit. He was the chief humanist of our wistful generation. Voltaire or Montaigne would have prized the light rhythm of his words: would have wondered perhaps by what irony he was American: would have seen the tortured body and read in it a symbol.

Randolph Bourne was the essayist of our time whose future must have been most worthy to stand with that of Brooks. In his college days, Bourne was a pragmatist—an intellectual. He sat at the feet of Professor Dewey. But the war, which drove all the world including Dewey mad, drove Bourne sane. The crisis which

* Born in Bloomfield, New Jersey, in 1886. Died in New York in December, 1918.

set and fixed the master, freed Bourne and made him
fluent. He who had sat among the rationalists now
turned to destroy them. Better than another, he knew
the blandishments of this practical philosophy. He
saw the lack of desire, the lack of life, understood what
catalepsy of the spirit Pragmatism meant to a groping nation. And while the American State moved with
the dead precision of a machine along the track of its
pioneer exploiters—a machine oiled by the intellectuals who were nothing but its slaves—Bourne rose to the
attack.

Such essays as *Below the Battle, War and the Intellectuals, Twilight of Idols* marked the literary voice
of young America, stirring at last against the iron
course upon which the old America had bound it.
Bourne found himself a leader of tens of thousands.
But they whom he led were silent and were scattered:
they whom he opposed were the Herd, with all the machinery of the world behind them. *The Seven Arts*, in
which Bourne had spoken, foundered. The other papers
shut their doors to him. During the last year, he made
a living, reviewing unworthy novels, waiting for the
Dawn. And as it broke, he died. . . .

. . . .

The best significance of Randolph Bourne lies in the
joining, through his work, of the political and the cultural currents of advance. Brooks holds aloof from
the transience of affairs. Our most sensitive poets and
novelists do likewise. The crassness of the American
world is too much for them. Unlike the European
lands, where all the activities of life and thought are

fused into that integer called Culture, Life in America is still a secluded, almost a romantic thing. The world is a Machine. To find the Life on which the artist feeds, he must withdraw from the Machine. He has done so. And conversely, the propagandist, the political rebel whose immediate concern is the Machine, withdraws from Life, from its immediate expressions which are religious and artistic. Bourne, almost alone, embraced the two. More than any of our fellows, he pointed the path of fusion which American leadership must take. His political discussions were actually lit by a spiritual viewpoint. They took into account the content of the human soul, the individual soul, the values of *being*. Through him, men who had lost touch with the spiritual base of life were led in its direction, since his discussions upon actual events, his discussions of the Machine, furnished a channel they could follow.

It is deep pity Randolph Bourne is dead. Our ranks were scant enough and straggling before he left them. Now, the political field is once more clearer to the pat materialist, the shallow liberal, the isolated radical whom he despised, and whom, eventually, his power of irony must have shamed. With him gone, the political and artistic columns of advance—Life and the Machine—are again severed.

This state of confusion and disarray runs through the entire intellectual world of our metropolis. Everywhere it is clear that America is still in the chaotic stage of individual effort: the individualism of the unintegrated herd as contradistinguished from that of the social unit. To step out from the Lump means to find ourselves alone. Group life on the level of young America still fails. Only the Opposition is close-knit. Millionaire and journalist and politician, venal author and the serf-hordes of Business know each other's mind, corroborate each other's word. On their dark level, which has become a level of defense, there is unity indeed. But in the scattered corners of the great Darkness, many men light many fitful fires. When once they meet, a flame will blaze across the sky.

VIII. THE MULTITUDES IN WHITMAN

THE one true hierarchy of values in the world is the hierarchy of Consciousness. Most men stir about upon their little plane and know it badly. They are gnats gliding the surface of a pond. Some men's knowing holds three dimensions. They see the flat world they act in: but they know it to be a facet of a greater world, and thereby they know it better. Countries, continents perhaps, the tangled traffic of peoples and of men, come in to them. But there are souls whose consciousness is higher. They partake of this global, three-dimensioned world, but know it too for a mere moving surface, moving beyond itself into dimensions that are truer, and that cease from motion as they become more true.

These are the great mystics. Such a one was Whitman. He saw the movements of men upon the flat planes of mundane life in its relation to all mundane life. He saw the unitary flow of all mundane life in its relation to an infinite Being of which it was an elementary part. He saw, though he could never understand, the *immediate* solution of each finite act in infinite fixity.

In this vast vista, only, may we behold Walt Whitman. In this proportion, he addressed the common prostitute:

"Not till the sun excludes you, do I exclude you;
Not till the waters refuse to glisten for you, and the
    leaves to rustle for you, do my words refuse to
    glisten and to rustle for you."

In this proportion, sang:

"Evil propels me and reform of evil propels me——
I moisten the roots of all that has grown."

For the song of Whitman's vision was the orchestra
of life. The Word of Whitman's vision was a perfect
sea, and in the sea a world, and in the world all men.
To cavil at his form is simply to fall short of his ulti-
mate vision, to fail of being caught in the sweeping
rhythm of his consciousness.

The critics, therefore, who interpret Whitman as
"father of social revolution," "father of free verse,"
"father of the American tongue," "propagandist of
American cultural liberation" dangerously reduce him.
He was these things. But he was far more. To call
him American in the sense of explanation is to reduce
him also. Little men and little groups hack at the
mighty figure and take their chip and cry: "Behold our
poet!" Let us not do likewise.

The whole world can claim Walt Whitman best. To
draw the men whom we have drawn has been to draw
America. Whitman is implicit in their aspiration. His
light shines in their lives: his work lives in their up-
ward-moving. To draw Walt Whitman straight would
bring us upon visions of a world in God whose boundaries converge with the vision of the Hindus, join the

dominions of Isaiah and David. And such purpose this
book has not.

Yet we are right to know and to recall that this
man was born among us: that he never left our lands.
He talked with God, standing upon America as Moses
upon Sinai. He talked with God, speaking our tongue.
America therefore is holy land to us. Not because
Whitman stood upon it, but because we have faith that
there is meaning in the fact that Whitman stood upon
it. Because we cannot be so weak as to doubt that in
this juncture of his spirit and our land is revelation.

.   .   .   .   .   .

When we have apperceived the *form*, the *density* of
Whitman's vision—and only then—we may dwell safely
upon that surface of it which was America. The specific naming of America in his work has for a generation thrown his well-wishers out of understanding. But
in the larger synthesis it becomes invaluable to our
search for an American ideal.

"*I am large—I contain multitudes,*" he sang. And
the multitudes of whom he dreamed, whom he dreamed
to mother, were Americans. As with Moses again, a
deep unconscious impulse made the transfer from his
own election, to his people. Since he was chosen, his
was a chosen people.

Whitman's great prose work, *Democratic Vistas*, is
full of considerations of this choice. In 1871, when it
appeared, his true Song was ended. Now he turns to
the scrutiny of this particular, actual corner of the
Globe whence his Song rose, of this particular lot of
human beings for whom it was particularly intended.

Democratic Vistas is quite as clearly our greatest book of social criticism as *Leaves of Grass* is our greatest poem. All of Emerson is pale and shredded and remote beside the immediacy of this mighty prose. "I am large—I contain multitudes," sang the poet. We know what he meant. Societies of luminous men, of loving women, multitudes who create, multitudes who know and live. Now, in his prose afterthought, "Let us have a look at *this* multitude we have," he seems to say. He understands the tragical discrepancy between the vision and the unquickened matter. He understands how far the fire must burn down to make luminous the whole. But he dies undismayed.

That was in 1892. Where, now, are the multitudes in Whitman?

Scarcely a generation of man since Whitman died. Can a new and unexampled race of multitudes be born in scarce one man's generation? Are we not still, not only at the point of Whitman's last wistful looking, but even of his first passionate scrutiny, in 1871?

If we hold our faces close to the scattered fires, as we have done deliberately in this book, we glow. But if we withdraw into the encompassing darkness, we must feel how pathetically short has been our coming on, since Whitman, also, turned his face from the flame of his own Vision to the blackness of his world.

. . . .

Nothing can be more sure than the spontaneous births of creative impulse in individual men and women throughout America. How do they thrive?

America had looser days. There was an America

not yet so closely bound in its straitjacket of steel rails and electric wires, but that much individual life came to a sort of social articulation. Sectionalism had its hour. East and West, South and North, mountain-land and plain were forced into the independence of their isolation. And upon their formlessness individual intellects of many kinds took form. The Civil War, in its defeat of the great Southern Sectionalism, marked the downfall of eccentric growths: marked the rise of a new knitting process—Capitalist Industrialism—against which the scattered shoots of American cultural expression could not prevail.

American journalism had been a hardy youngster. Papers flourished in every corner, whose will and accent and color were determined by that corner. Whitman himself was an editor! Famous journals like the *New York Tribune*, the *New York Sun*, the *Boston Transcript*, the *Springfield Republican*, the *Louisville Courier-Journal*, the *Portland Oregonian*, the *Omaha Bee*, the *Chicago Tribune*, the *Detroit Free Press*, the *Cleveland Plain Dealer*, the *New Orleans Picayune* gave a counterpoint of voices to the several states. Editors in those days were personages. Their organs articulated local life. They were vigorous, self-assertive, often delightful in the quirks and oddities of sectional feeling.

Then, the Syndicate came into being. By its benign economy, scores of papers in scores of cities appear each day with the same countenance. New York clerk, Illinois farmer, Colorado miner, fisherman from the Columbia River take the same journalistic food into their heads. For the Syndicate is a factory. It manufactures news, cartoons, poetry, fiction, sermons on life, special articles, dramatic criticism, editorial opinion—in standard forms. These commodities it pours by its electric sluices over the wide American lands. With the result that the local newspaper is practically dead. Lima, Ohio, Phoenix, Arizona, Augusta, Maine, publish merely local editions of syndicated "news."

These huge organizations of course command money, which is another way of saying that money commands them. They are the products of Capitalism. They are not disloyal. They do not deny their Maker. Every word of "news," every line of a cartoon, every moralistic squib that they conduit forth sounds with worship of the Power that controls them: strengthens the hold of organized materialism: blots out by the simple process of ignoring or of falsifying any more than modest growth in the vast land which seems inimical to the continued reign of Money.

The American is the world's greatest reader of journalistic matter. He has no peasant or guild background. The articulations of craft and music mean little to him. He is dependent on the Printed Word. And the Printed Word that he receives comes at least indirectly from a single source. And that source immune from any vision, thought, the cognizance of any fact, hostile to its industrial Progenitor.

What is true of the journal is of course true likewise of the magazine and the published volume. Only great companies can command the publicity and salesmanship needed to distribute wares over the areas of the United

States. These capacities mean vast expense: mean close relationship with our socialized financial system.

Behold the vicious circle of Puritan Industrialism! Here is a magazine with a circulation of a million. It sells for five or ten cents—a mere fraction of its actual printing cost, to say nothing of the cost of shipping it to the sparse centers of a continent. It carries a hundred pages of advertisements which, in good sooth, "carry" the magazine. The vast circulation justifies the great prices paid by the advertisers. These justify the cheapness of its cost to the readers. And the cheapness assures the circulation and the bulk of advertisements. The magazine may go from New York to the remotest corner of Alaska and undersell any local print. It ransacks the world for attractive and high-sounding matter and then offers it to the public for a song. It is a mere decked-out carrier for advertisers. And these advertisers form part, of course, of the Industrial machine which all America, even in its moments of relaxation, must therefore serve.

The effect of this perfect system is widespread. Provincial expression is wiped out by the metropolitan inspiration of "news" and literary matter. The great cities are dumb before the need of determining what they shall say by the standards of acceptibility in Kansas and New Hampshire. Province and metropolis neutralize and denature one another. The small town paper lives by its syndicated "news." But the Syndicates live by the small town paper. There must be no offense, one way or the other. The budget of a great New York daily demands that its high-paid talent produce syndicable matter. A cartoonist who might conceivably please Chicago but who offends the good people of Tulsa, Oklahoma, will soon be jobless.

Thus the whole country has been debased to a lowest common denominator of expression. The Machine and the money that it produces have become the true currency of word, ideal and thought. Against this condition rise the solitary voices we have heard—the utterance of great and hardy souls. They crave an audience. But the multitude who might naturally catch their meaning is too enslaved and enfeebled by the poisonous pabulum with which Business persistently has fed it. Adulterate journals, specious magazines, widely touted, saccharinated novels stuff it too full. The solitary voices seek each other out across the American wastes, and no one else attends them.

Universities have immemorially been breeders of rebellious groups. In America, for the most part, they are incubators of reaction. Another triumph of the Commercial system. Our schools and colleges were largely founded by Puritans and pioneers. To-day, they are endowed by the successors of these: the industrial masters. The wreathing tendency of Capitalism to centralize production has long since taken them in. Production of knowledge, production of faith are now controlled equally with production of information and amusement. The recent crisis of the War must have made this clear to those remaining persons who still believed in the myths of American free thought and American free speech. Teachers were thrown peremptorily out of public schools not alone for socialistic teaching but for the mere desire to record in their classes, or otherwise, certain facts—notably concerning Russia. Professors in leading universities found themselves suddenly in the streets because of a liberal attitude toward social change. It became clear at once that the Academic powers of America were willing to go to the length of open persecution to check the possible growth of active minorities of youth armed in faith and knowledge against the moneyed classes that ruled America.*

So here again, the rightful progress of our spiritual leaders to an audience is barred. Every nerve of the American controlling organism strains against the life of liberal thought and revolutionary faith: against the cult of any beauty that is not slavish and minor. Whitman and his sons cry for their multitudes to be born anew: and the American powers take every step to preserve them in a state of ignorance, flatulence, complacency which shall approximate the Herd.

And this is precisely what in America has taken place. A high average of individual integrity comes only with great social growth: partakes of the nature

* Constructive reaction against these conditions has already set in, in New York. "The New School for Social Research," recently founded, is a first move toward a free university. The lecturers of this free promising institution are largely leading professors who have left their established universities because of the impossibly illiberal conditions. They include such men as James Harvey Robinson, author of *The New History;* Charles A. Beard, author of *An Economic Interpretation of the Constitution of the United States;* Thorstein Veblen, author of *A Theory of the Leisure Class, An Inquiry into the Nature of Peace,* and possibly America's foremost social philosopher; Harold J. Laski, etc.

of social integration. But as we have seen, cultural individuation died with the birth of the pioneer. Man was once more leveled downward. Self-governing and self-seeking persons poured into America. But they found no Eden. Nature and men were hostile: Europe and the outlying worlds. They needed therefore to become a group: to their own preservation, to their own material advancement. They needed to come together, as the first men had done, and as their first instincts, to which they had gone back, suggested. And so, in truth, they did come together. With the long process of social integration far above them. As a *herd*.

The traditional democracy of the United States is a disguised ideal of the herd. "Every man for himself, and the devil take the hindmost." "I am as good as you, and a damn sight better." "Any man is fit to become president." So the herd-rubrics run. Let me explain by a crude instance.

Two thousand sheep crop the steep greenness of a Wyoming hill. The herder has one dog. With his snout low, feeling the passion of his game, the splendid brute skirts the left flank of the tumultuous, billowy unit, snapping, growling, running swift: and the scared sheep, touched in their social sense, veer madly to the right. The dog has brushed a score of them. But his will runs through them all. Two thousand sheep swerve to his will, as if he held each one of them in leash. So the dog pours the flock into the hollow where it is to rest for the night: each sheep tremulous, marvelously quick to his far command, quite as the whole horse bounds when a whip flecks his ear. . . . The herder has a guest to supper. He decides on a feast. He takes his gun and strides into the thick of the flock, seeking a dry ewe to slaughter. The sheep feel no call from him, no danger. They graze. The herder has to kick them aside. He finds his ewe. He takes her by the throat and discharges his gun against her heart. The mountains shriek with the explosion. The ewe collapses, bloody. The other sheep, packed close about the murder, go on tranquilly grazing.

So the social consciousness of old America. Nervous, hypersensitive in response to the disturbance that menaces it as a whole: deaf to the fate of individual components. A true herd reaction. It will give heed to the low call of the papers, the call to the passions and hungers of the pack: give heed though the call send it regularly to be shorn and slaughtered. But to the voice of the poet and the artist it is deaf. The mental food which it receives in school and church and newspaper and "show" has its regressive virtue. No multitudes as yet, in Whitman.

. . . .

Perhaps this lack is nowhere clearer than in the condition of our social arts. The Theater, for instance.

Roughly, there are three theaters in the United States: the popular Theater, the bourgeois Theater which is synonymous with Broadway, and the "intellectual" or "little" Theater of which scores have had their fitful hour during the past five years in scores of cities.

The popular Theater is largely the motion-picture.

In cities like New York, still unassimilated cultural groups—Jewish, Italian, German—have their play-houses where dramas, actors, audiences meet on a common mental and emotional level. Here, the naïver forms of the dramatic art still thrive: melodrama that is sincere, musical shows that are fresh, curious *mélanges*, like those of the Yiddish stage, where Synagogic chants merge with the latest ragtime of Broadway. These performances often surprise by their value. From under the shoddy surface of the plot come gleams of folk-lore, racial confessionals to clash with the cheap *patter* of the American assimilation. The whole immigrant drama stands out revealed in its pathos: one leaves, wondering how this period of transition could ever have remained so sweet under the towering harshness of American life. But of course this type of theater will disappear. It is a remnant that must be gone in the great process of absorption.

Until such time, however, the American who is hungry for dramatic health may go to the Yiddish and German* theaters and somewhat be appeased. It is here, not on Broadway, that the European masters, classic and modern, receive competent attention. Shakespeare and Shaw, Tolstoi and Chekov, Ibsen, Strindberg, Schnitzler recur constantly on Yiddish and German playbills. And they are presented with amazing fidelity and power. The companies are largely recruited from old-world capitals: always they are schooled in a true tradition that is unknown in the An-

---

* Since our participation in the War, of course, the German theaters have been closed.

glo-Saxon countries. And they are supported by audiences similarly schooled: receptive and respectful before dramatic art. In fact, the entire phenomenon devolves upon the audience. As the public becomes more totally Americanized, this vital relic stage will disappear.

The true popular Theater of the American masses is, thus, the Movie. Before the Movie, the American masses had no theater. The whole world now has its cinemas. America alone has nothing else. America alone has nothing better.

Charlie Chaplin meets America on the one level where it can be sincere: speaks to America in terms which it best understands, since they are essentially its own. Charlie Chaplin is therefore our most significant and most authentic dramatic figure. Within the cultural limitations imposed upon him by his public, he is a perfect artist. Inimitably graceful, mobile of body and feature, capable of a kaleidoscopic scale of feeling, from tears to laughter, from "rough-house" to the most delicate mimic dance, where is his equal in our dramatic world? The theater may become a group expression when we have a group. It is a herd expression in a herd. The theater of Chaplin springs doubtless from this low social base. But it rises naturally, organically. Therefore it is good.

Gaiety, adventure, the sweet extravagance of romance—such are the loves of men which in America have been suppressed. In Chaplin they bob up. He is a capering, electric sprite, expressing in tomfoolery and laughter the serious beauties which America else-

wise may not approach. His art is simple, poetic, because of the longings it responds to. It is infantile
because of the deep repression. It is fluent and elusive,
because these qualities of life have as yet no form in
our world.

There are sophistications in Chaplin's work that are
not healthy. It must be borne in mind that he strad-
dles the theatric worlds: and that repressed emotions
are at best an ugly business. But there is social criticism in his antics: and of a sort far deeper than the
multitudes who laugh may know. Much of his upset-
ting of conventions—a parlor full of brocaded ladies
suddenly pelted with cream-puffs, a stodgy vaudeville
show suddenly made exciting as the audience breaks out
and makes a show for itself—points to the mere uncon-
fessed desire of healthy men and women who are cowed
by a ponderous Middle-Class. His comedy, *Shoulder
Arms*, was a real satire upon the absurdity of war, in
terms at which even the Censor had to laugh but which
conveyed, no less, the reactions of a sensitive spirit to
the vicious pomposity of modern Warfare.

There is no doubt: Chaplin is our sweetest playboy,
our classic clown, sprite of our buried loves. He is
at once the Puck and the muse of a harried people who
find in his antic loveliness a mirror for their own wistful and forbidden gaiety, a glimmering invitation to
respite and abandon.

Leaving Charlie Chaplin we leave the sole radiance
of the American theater. We founder upon the ugly
sophistications of what Randolph Bourne has called

the "significant classes"—classes with no further mission in the world than to be destroyed.

The Broadway theater may have its like in drooping ages of the past. If so, I have not found it. The tales of "Petronius," for instance, possibly herald the Roman cataclysm. I do not know. But I do know that they are instinct with grace and art. They are the last words of a world at least unashamed of beauty, that erred only in too far saying "Yea." The Broadway stage is the last doddering ejaculation of a Class that erred otherwise, of a Class that we know already: they who denied life, stringently, with philosophy and system—the children of Puritan and Pioneer.

Quite literally, the Theater of Broadway is the Theater of the whole American Middle-Class. The trains pour in the buying and selling multitudes from Florida and the Mississippi and the West. It is this vapid, vacant, shifting throng of spending men and women— loosed for a week from the humdrum of their lives— who fill the theaters. And it is the same plays, one or three seasons later, that visit their less prosperous brethren in the provincial cities.

I prefer not to dwell here on the content of the Broadway "shows." The American Middle-Class could never, by its origins and precepts, have become a vital spiritual force, like the burghers of European cities. But even in America, it did produce certain creditable forms. The old brownstone houses that still stand in certain portions of Boston, Chicago, Brooklyn and Manhattan attest an honesty and health that their more sumptuous successors lack. Colonial architecture, both North and South, achieved a splendid and independent, if fleeting beauty. And much of the furniture of old America, while plainly derived from English models, was gracefully expressive—until the *Empire* forms debauched it forevermore. So also, America had a stage tradition: we produced good actors. Also, we produced melodrama, burlesque (like *Weber and Fields*, and *Harrigan and Hart*) which were indigenous and lusty. The audiences believed in these "shows." They gave them a part of the native health which the Middle-Class still had. But now, all that is gone. The younger generation of theatergoers scarcely recalls the older caste of actors: seems satisfied with the feeble incompetents that take their place. The older generation of plays seeks a last refuge in the foreign-language theaters. They are deformed even in the movies. From Broadway, they have altogether passed.

The new plays are not even naïve, not even empty. They are rancid and blatantly false. They are not merely unlovely. They are the assertion of all that is hideous and perverse in the submerged life of a Class which has denied life for generations and which besides, by the fatal accident of wealth, is removed from even those fortuitous living contacts which poverty—the common career of men—inevitably brings.

If the Broadway play can be said to have a hero he is the embodiment of the tricks of modern commerce. Broadway crowns the American *picaresque*. Broadway is populous with charming crooks. The audiences never cease from thrilling at the antics of clever manipulators of other people's money. Get-

217

Rich-Quick-Wallingford succeeds Sir Galahad. Once the Holy Grail—now Cash. Play follows play in which the penniless young man by hook and crook angles his way into the ranks of the millionaire. But always to the *obbligato* of "Puritan" precepts and a pure young lady. Such, the positive impulse of the Bourgeois drama: material possession. The negative impulse is of course sexual repression—the old Puritan formula with which we are familiar. Broadway festers with plays that are mere "peep-shows": its heroes of farce and musical comedy are *voyeurs*, with homosexual proclivities; its heroines are *frôleuses* or salamanders. The perverse makeshifts of desire must crowd the stage of a Class which is afraid of what is fertile.

Unfortunately, the third Theater—the "intellectual" Theater—of America is not basally separate from the bourgeois Theater of Broadway. The determinant in any theater is the audience. The health of William S. Hart with his childish tales of a mythical frontier, the health of Chaplin with his mimic genius, are but the health of the gaping, unspoiled multitudes that behold them. The purulence of Broadway is but the rot of an exploiting Class as it nears the term of its depleted life. The weakness of our "intellectual" Theater is fundamentally that it has no public to bring it into strength.

Here is a function for the multitude in Whitman! A function unfulfilled, since the multitude remains unborn.

There have been scores of these little theaters. Possibly—I suspect so—those in the West have been less

impotent than those which I have studied in New York.
But although their level of production may have been
less low, their audiences perhaps less vitiate and sodden, they too have produced no good American plays.
As an editor I have at least read many of the plays
they gave, though I did not see them acted. Uniformly,
they have been weak: imitations of European styles,
jejune, unvital.

A theater without an audience is as unthinkable as
a painting without paint. A man may write a good
novel, sing a fair song in the dark. Many men have
done just that, as we have seen, throughout America.
He cannot produce a theater without an audience. For
the multitude is the pigment of the dramatic picture.

So do I explain the failure of significant Americans
for the most part to work in the theater. At least two
such men, Theodore Dreiser and Robert Frost, have
written plays. Good plays: almost, I think, the only
good plays we have. But these men take no part in
the much-noised, much-agitative "little theater" movements. Unconsciously, they moved to means that were
at hand to express their bursting vision. To speak
through a theater, they needed to have a group: and
worthy group there is not.

The little theaters of New York have been largely
in the hands of half-serious, half-competent men. Men
in whom all the vices of the Broadway stage were
grounded. They have leaned halfway to Europe for
tricks of dramaturgy—Maeterlinck and Shaw and
Synge and Schnitzler, and for tricks of presentation—
Reinhardt and Gordon Craig. They have leaned a lit-

tle more than halfway to the dull, spoiled audiences of Broadway for their needed realization. Often, they have produced good foreign plays: always badly: frequently to the delight of a flattered multitude which could pay.

I do not in the least blame the leaders of these little Theaters. They are not conscientious artists: they are not even competent workers: they seem to lack the respect for craft and loveliness of the average unspoiled child. Doubtless, they do their best. . . . But is not the emergence of such people in our social arts a natural consequence of our acquisitive, mechanical culture? Not everybody can know how to act, nor how to select and produce good drama. What is important, is that just such ungifted and unseeing ones as these should to-day command our "intellectual" theaters. And this is important because it is the inevitable expression of the audience that in reality commands these theaters.

When we possess a multitude, however small a multitude, who have reverence for life, a margin of energy for living, understanding of the sacrament of life's interpretation, we shall beget critics of conscionable taste. And at once, men and women in whom the love of beauty is a creative force will come in at the stage door and complete the work.*

.   .   .   .

* The isolation of the great abilities of Robert Edmond Jones may perhaps be symbolically expressed by discussing him outside the brief text which I have devoted to the non-existent intellectual Theater. Jones is a scenic artist, master of *mise-en-scène,* with true gifts of lyrical creation in color and plastic composi-

Let us step out from the American theaters into the streets of American life. . . .

These clamorous buildings drip energy. This iron world is a tissue of complex human wills. Underneath, walks the multitude: colorless, cowed, the abject creature of its creation. But this delirium of stone, for all its seeming mastery, is but a scum on the energies of men. The multitude has better powers. Can it not build higher than these buildings?

tion. What his full powers are, I do not know, for he has had no real working chance to show them. With excellent intuition, Jones has gradually diverged from the little theaters and taken up his work with the professional Broadway stage. When Granville Barker was in New York, Jones blossomed forth. Barker left no substitute of atmosphere or background. Our intellectual theaters have most of the vices and emptinesses of their big brother, the bourgeois theater: and they lack the occasional competence of what is at least traditional and professional. The bourgeois theater is the expression of a dying Class: but at least that Class exists. It has the solidity of existence. The intellectual theater depends upon a hypothetic multitude which is not alive enough even to be dying. In a way, Jones is a tragedy. He has ideals, vision, energy, a tremendous and unsated instinct for social craft. His mind teems with creation. He has neither dramatist nor audience to work with. This last season, for instance, he wasted his poesy upon Sem Benelli: and misapplied it upon Tolstoi's *Living Corpse,* for which his temperament unfitted him. Jones is a lyrist, a romantic colorist. There is the hand of the insouciant sun-god upon his best creations. But no good work is being done for him in America at all: and most of the good work of Europe during the past epoch has been sombre, realistic, analytic: the very antithesis of his own gay humor. The gaiety and color of Jones are more than literary: they are real. It must be avowed that he breathed a true song even into Sem Benelli. His lyrism insists on singing in a cloudy world. If he does not lose heart, perhaps a newer generation will bring a reason to his indomitable laughter.

IX. THE TURNING OF THE SOIL

PROBABLY there can be no such thing as an irreligious people. The need of men for knowledge of their fellowship with Life may be in part converted to immediate and compelling ends: the rest repressed. But the need prevails—the Source that forever casts it up. And in good time, it speaks. So, at the climax of the Nineteenth Century spoke Lincoln and Walt Whitman. So, now. . . .

In 1855, the first song of the Poet. In 1867 *Drum-Taps* closed the full-throated utterance. Lincoln was dead in 1865. Twelve years of apocalypse. The nadir of a Century of mad immersion in affairs. And at the nadir, this apparition of two men of God.

Then, their mystery sank down. The storm of greed swirled higher. For forty years its black beat across our land was almost monotone. Unrivaled. The hearts and spirits of men and women flew before the blast of material aggrandizement like chaff of winnowed wheat. The grain was the gold.

At last, voices of protest and positive desire. Feeble, they were swallowed up in the roar of commerce. Men like William Jennings Bryan whom America has learned to sneer at: lyrical but ignorant, crying against the tramp of a State toward its imperialistic goal, vaguely wistful for social justice and for a quality of life he could not name since he had never known it. Bryan was a voice without a mind. Speaking in 1896, as if Karl Marx had never lived. No schools to teach him a way of winning his thin dream: also no minds about to receive his words and turn them into thought. Bryan failed to become President. Even if he had succeeded, he must have failed. He spoke against the momentum of a world. . . . The Spanish War sharpened the claws of the American Eagle: sharpened his scope and his greed. Roosevelt rose to power upon the whirlwind Bryan had tried to stay.

Meantime, a younger world was trying to grow up. The gods of the fathers were ridiculous or dead. So the young world was godless. The forces of the fathers had been poured out upon the chaos of a ruthless continent. So the young world was weary.

Mechanical progress split life into myriad mechanical departments. Every machine had a thousand parts. Every calling had a thousand machines. Newspaper and technical school and telegraph and telephone loaded the average mind with a surfeit of details to be mastered for the making of money. The inevitable came. "Man by nature desires to know," said Aristotle. In most men perhaps a weak desire. But in the long ages of the world, when Nature stood fairly near to man, when no elaborate tools and structures towered about him, this desire turned direct to the nearest things: to contemplation of the values of life and nature, to the immanence of God, to the passion of beauty. These, then, were knowledge, and so Aristotle —so Dante—used the word. But now, the new multitude of fact and of detail deluged man's mind; shut him away from the eternal contemplations, so that at first he denied them, later forgot them. America offered the unique human spectacle: a people brilliant and strong, in whom the desire to *know* seemed actually to have died!

Only the thought and deed which lead man to the sources of life are the life-givers. Broken from these conduits, he becomes the most helpless of particles in a buffeting world. His superior mental scope serves merely to destroy him. For it lets in an infinitude of facts, and he is under them; they overwhelm him. Only in the consciousness of life as a Whole, in the consciousness of himself as a parabolic force with his feet upon earth and his head piercing the skies—the consciousness which all religions in their own ways preserve, all arts express—can man prevail against the clutter of a factual and emotional multiverse. . . . Now, America multiplied this clutter: America took away the consciousness that might have held it.

No wonder, then, that so many children of the Pioneer were weary: that so much of their behavior and thought goes back to weariness. The young pragmatist surrendered to the developed rhythm of his country: applied his superior mentality to rationalize surrender. Because he was weary. The young materialist shut out the infinite conduits of sense and thought that lead to Mystery, that silence Reason: huddled in his little room of fact denying the rest. Because he was weary. The young liberal rebelled against the disorder of the world his fathers had bequeathed him, and now re-

belled once more against the new world that is breaking, since it too was breaking in bloodshed and disorder. Because he craved comfort. Because he was
weary. The young artist shut out the brutal and
overwhelming day from his desire: spun pretty spider-
webs of fancy, or escaped to the hothouses of Europe
where he thought *his* world would become distant and
unreal: or huddled with his kind in the Bohemian quar-
ters of New York, warming thin blood with the heat
and the praise of others. Because he was weary. The
young partisan of social revolution, freed of the political myths, could free himself no further: remained
still subject to the spiritual Puritan negation: denied
beauty, denied God, hoped to swing over the idolatry
of the Machine to a new Order, not understanding how
his failure to plunge to the source of energy and life
frustrated his effort at the outset. Because he too was
weary. And the others—the broad-girthed, deep-
souled masters whom America throws up from her
chaos—clambered to consciousness, sent out their
voices. But even in them much of the power that
should have swelled their song had gone from them like
blood in their ceaseless battle for release from a mastering, denying world. So that they were weary
also. . . .

America was full of beauty and strength which
marching America had trampled. The material March
went on. It had been the premise of American life. It
moved to its irresistible conclusion: upon War.

It had cleared the continent. It had become the impulse of the modern World. Europe was given up to

it. But Europe had a past. The possessive passion
was turmoiled and thwarted in Europe by ancient loves
that slept in the blood but were not dead. In America, the possessive passion was more perfect. For
America was the child of its first great adventure in the
Fifteenth Century. So now, in Europe, the system of
material acquisition reeled to the chaos that inhered
in it. The antiquated forms fell first: the Kaisers and
the Czars. The Western Democracies—later elabora-
tions—proved more enduring. The Westernmost was
the least alloyed. At the final act, America rushed to
France: Woodrow Wilson left Washington for Paris.
But already, in the East where the Old World had first
gone down, the new World had risen.

America in War felt the quickening of travail. Its
task of saving the old World had the effect of making
every phase of its life intenser. We were like a sim-
mering pot of water over a heightening fire, without
outlet. Each molecule of our social substance became
more agitant, became the carrier of greater force. The
Puritan and the pioneer scented the great game of the
old orders on the fields of Europe: the rebel found himself responding in advance to the sacrament of death
which he knew must be the harbinger of birth. The
old Order tightened its grip. The New prepared more
consciously for battle. The years of suspense had
drawn the lines more closely, made the colors clear.
America went into the fray with the cries of triumph
hot upon the lips of all who were dying in the world:
dying and inordinately active: the Capitalist and his
slave-orders, the European snob, the belated Colonial,

the suppressed lover of blood. And with each cry, young America came to understand. Silent and attentive, we were finding our own voice.

.   .   .   .

The vague process of coördinate advance has had its generation. We have watched its spontaneous unanimity in New York, New England, the vast Midland whose Capital is Chicago. We might have watched it likewise in other sections: Saint Louis or San Francisco where already twenty years ago, Frank Norris and Ambrose Bierce were making their barbaric and brave books. Now, with the War, the process is no longer vague. The open hands of pleading Youth harden to fists.

In Russia, the oppressive system permitted no careers in the open world to men's need of service and of creation. There was vast spiritual force in Russia. It was not allowed to grapple with reality. All cultural leaders of old Russia were therefore revolutionists. In America, the condition is reversed. Here is a land stocked with careers—empty of spirit: a land so harried by the cumulative press of actual affairs and by the Puritan philosophy which these affairs have fixed that no spiritual force can come to birth in it. An intricate and oppressive system perpetuates our fatal inequation quite as it did in Russia. Wherefore, all our cultural leaders are revolutionists, as well. The trouble is, that not all our revolutionists have been cultural leaders.

But at last, this betters also. New groups of well-equipped and intellectual athletes, schooled and traveled, take the lead in the stern and ugly business of social warfare. A liberal of the old American tradition like Oswald Garrison Villard is able, in the face of the new reality, to rise above that old tradition, and at the same time bring its equipment and integrity to bear upon the needed radicalism of to-day. A poet like Max Eastman turns his lyrism to propaganda. A critic like Floyd Dell interprets the social impulse of æsthetic work to minds that are eager but are still not æsthetically quickened. Cartoonists like Boardman Robinson, Robert Minor, Arthur Young bring their mastering love, their power of succinct analysis to the nascent revolution. A romantic figure like John Reed covers the battlefields of Europe watching for the birth he knows is due, serves Lenine in Russia, helps foment rebellion in Imperial Germany, and then returns to New York with the vision of transfiguration in his eyes. The Old Guard—martyrs like Eugene Debs, William Haywood, Emma Goldman—religious, nostalgic for prisons—find at last the brains and culture of a younger generation to fertilize their martyrdom.

And in the direct column of advance, poets and artists still swarm in from farm and provincial city. Anonymous, uncertain: but the best poets and the greatest artists doubtless among them.* Their bulk

---

* I regret that the physical limitations of this book keep me from individually discussing many poets, many critics, several novelists, whose places seem sure in the American promise. Slowly, painfully, America moves toward the period where artists converge into groups. Loose groups, as a rule, the best of which protest they are no groups at all: but generative of the

shall be resistless. They make loam for the growing prairie. The materialism of the middle-generation falls back to the despair that gave it birth. Like the materialism of Bazarov, it did its destructive work. It burned down the stubble of ancient harvests: it cleared the field for the new planting. The soil stands ready to be turned.

.   .   .   .

During a hundred years of her material existence, America succeeded. Success meant suppression of life: we have seen to what measure. The man who dreamed, loved, created rather than possessed, was a byword and a pariah. Life retreated—its mystery and infinite passion—to the domain of Failure.

In Failure, Life dwelt and survived. In Failure, the new prophets found it. The highest singers of our day —in prose or verse or pigment—are the singers of the holiness of failure. They have taught the American youth in what rags, what hovel, to seek his Beloved. They have taught the American youth the sanctity of Failure.

And then, with the War, Failure became a fact! Germany was crushed. But even the humble soldier, pulled from his job and dropped into the trenches, is aware dimly that the whole structure of pat words, pat panaceas, pat utopias is crumbling. He understands the shrillness of politicians, of the conservative organs. Everywhere, he detects the accent of fear, and, look-

sort of energy that prods the half-awakened intellectual classes of our cities.

ing close, sees the immanence of a vast breaking-up. Society is rotten: the State is a pious criminal: the old truths are tawdry lies: the old promises that sent him cheering into War are precisely what his martial steps first battered down. Everywhere, is the impotence of senility. He slaps his thigh and finds that only he is sound. And who is he? That also he begins to understand. He is what America has immemorially denied: the dreamer, the lover. He is the failure. And he alone stands healthy above the crumble of worlds.

My soldier is still not numerous: not articulate. Give him time. He is the bringer of a new religion, he is the maker of multitudes. His day in America is not quite yet. The forces of recreation are still too scattered and scantily munitioned. The artist is still alone: his voice has not reverberated far. The call of the revolutionist is muffled. The message of the one and the message of the other do not yet converge on the same people. The men who listen to Stieglitz have not yet quite joined him in their mind with the example of Bill Haywood. And the readers of socialistic pamphlets have not heard of "291." In other words, the impulse of New America is still unfused. Unfused it cannot prevail against the entrenchment of the Old.

The material of the creative act is there. What waits is the creative impulse.

This impulse cannot be intellectual, must as its name implies, proceed from love. Love of life, love of *being*. In Europe it was never far submerged despite the blight of the Nineteenth Century upon it. The mystical experience of Russia nursed the people through centuries of oppression: bore the will at last to throw them up into the light. Heaven was transferred from death to life. Revolution followed with logical precision. All of the peasant and proletarian peoples of Europe have this deep potential energy—religious, æsthetic—which is simply the love of life and which, applied by suffering and education to the level of practical demands, becomes indefeasibly the kinetic energy of revolt.

Here, America, of all lands, is poorest. Already two hundred years ago, American energy had become external: fled equally from the soil of the land and from the soul of man. We had no ancient tenancies to breed mellowness and contemplation. We had no fixed traditions upon which the soul could fall back and rest and gather strength. From the beginning we were a people centrifugal, nervous, impatient. No potential energy could store in us: we poured ourselves unendingly, pioneering and exploiting. The crisis finds us to-day, innerly depleted. We are clever. We are literate. We are materially advanced. But, facing the mandate of our hour, the recreation of a world, we are more backward than the Magyar or the Slav, because we lack that spiritual substance which creates Faith and which moves mountains.

This then is our task. Whitman foresaw it and sang of it and warned us. We must go through a period of static suffering, of inner cultivation. We must break our impotent habit of constant issuance into petty deed. We must begin to generate within ourselves the energy which is love of life. For that energy, to whatever form the mind consign it, is religious. Its act is creation. And in a dying world, creation is revolution.

THE END

.